T0156709

BELONGING EXPERIENCES

DESIGNING ENGAGED BRANDS

JEAN-PIERRE LACROIX

iUniverse, Inc.
New York   Bloomington

Belonging Experiences
Designing Engaged Brands

iUniverse books may be ordered through booksellers or by contacting:

iUniverse
1663 Liberty Drive
Bloomington, IN 47403
www.iuniverse.com
1-800-Authors (1-800-288-4677)

Because of the dynamic nature of the Internet, any Web addresses or links contained in this book may have changed since publication and may no longer be valid. .

ISBN: 978-1-4502-3051-3 (sc)
ISBN: 978-1-4502-3050-6 (dj)
ISBN: 978-1-4502-3049-0 (ebk)

Library of Congress Control Number: 2010907584

Printed in the United States of America

iUniverse rev. date: 5/28/2010

CONTENTS

With gratitude to my wife, Jo-Ann Lacroix; my daughter, Anne-Marie Lacroix; my devoted team at Shikatani Lacroix; the staff at Strategic Coach; and my supportive clients for showing me the way and providing support.

PREFACE

The nucleus for the concept of this book came to me while sitting through research being conducted for a large retail chain in the late 1990s. It became apparent that the growth of technology and shifts in the family structure have left consumers disconnected from daily social contacts and skeptical of product and service claims. This theme would continue to be expressed not only by experiential brands, such as banks and food service retailers, but also by consumable products ranging from pharmaceuticals to everyday household goods. Consumers are becoming overwhelmed by the multitude of offers and products being promoted and have become dubious and indifferent as a result.

I noticed a trend emerge from these challenges, where consumers were looking for brands to provide more than simply the functional benefits of their products and services. Consumers were looking for knowledge and understanding of how these brands could better their lives. As such, they wanted to be part of an experience that allowed them to be fully in control of and engaged in what the brand could offer as a reflection of their values and lifestyle needs. The proliferation of blogs and social networks has proven that this deep need has been ever-present and underserved. This book focuses on the underlying trends driving how consumers connect with brands and provides a new engagement model that leverages these trends to benefit marketers striving to build brand loyalty.

INTRODUCTION
CONNECTING THE MEANING

The term "Belonging Experiences" was born out of over three decades of experience working with some of the world's leading consumer packaged goods, service providers, and retail brands. From this unique vantage point, it became quite clear to me that the next decade would see a significant shift in how consumers interact with retail and service brands. The term clearly captures the essence of this change, articulated through the combination of two emotional words. The "Experience" is at one end of the spectrum, identified by its physical characteristics, such as the decor, atmosphere, and tangible offerings that predominantly stimulate the senses. This lays the foundation for giving permission to foster a transaction leading to a relationship.

At the other end of the spectrum, "Belonging" is a prevailing consumer need that is illustrated by the shift of power gradually occurring in the marketplace. It also encompasses the way leading marketers are leveraging a systematic approach to sharing this control with consumers in order to answer their need for empowerment and a strong sense of collaboration. The combination of these two dimensions provides a unique catalyst for consumers to collaborate, get engaged, and become advocates for your brand. The net benefit is a brand momentum that goes far beyond conventional marketing efforts and financial investments in maintaining brand loyalty.

As I write this book, my firm is currently working with leading organizations in the transformation of their physical assets or packaged goods brands into "Belonging Experiences" that leverage knowledge as the new currency. These projects support our belief in the need for experiences to evolve far beyond the approaches of past decades to a new level that builds on knowledge as the new foundation of the experience and true value of the brand.

CHAPTER ONE
SEEING AROUND THE CORNER

Marketers are entering a new decade where the only constant is change at lightning speed and the only reality is a market that is becoming blurred and fragmented. The challenge for marketers is daunting: How do I create strong brand loyalty when there is so much competition for customers' attention and needs? How do I ensure that my offering is relevant and meaningful when the shift of power is migrating to consumers and the approach I take to reach them is ever-changing? The factors now influencing how consumers connect with brands and the way marketers can best leverage key trends to ensure that their products and services are on the preferred list are the underlying issues that this report will take into consideration.

More importantly, the next opportunity that marketers of products and services need to consider when developing their marketing initiatives will be explored. The following pages will allow you to "see around the corner" in order to identify opportunities that the market has yet to capitalize on, while gaining a further understanding of what is driving these opportunities.

As we explore the opportunities that exist in creating a Belonging Experience, we will answer the following questions:

- What are the key factors that are shaping the way consumers interact with brands?
- How can brands leverage the key factors that drive brand loyalty?
- What organizations can we benchmark for key learning?
- What is the new Belonging Experience model, and how does it relate to the key market-driving factors?
- How does an organization create a Belonging Experience that works within its culture?

BRAND EXPERIENCE CONTINUUM

The next decade, I believe, will bring about a major shift in how marketers create value and brand loyalty within a hypercompetitive, ever-confusing marketplace. In order to better understand what opportunities are just around the corner, it is important to understand how the market has evolved in the past two decades. If we look back, the 1990s was the decade of emotional branding. Organizations embarked on identifying an optimum brand position in consumers' minds that went far beyond functional benefits. This shift was created out of an understanding that consumers' lifestyle needs were evolving. Marketers had to shift their communication from a rational perspective to encompass new emotional values that were lifestyle-driven in order to effectively market to them.

Marketers had come to understand that the way brands connected with consumers on the emotional level had a significant impact on brand loyalty and intent to purchase. The rise of mass affluence driven by increased discretionary dollars and the need for style popularized by design-centric television shows evolved as a means to embody this new trend. Self-image and style continues to play an important role in how consumers perceive brands. Even in times of economic uncertainty and financial crisis, the consumer need to indulge and buy brands that reflect their values continues to prosper and thrive.

DECADE OF THE EXPERIENTIAL BRAND

In the decade that followed, the rise of the Internet as both an alternative channel of distribution for marketers as well as a medium to share and spread information forced many marketers to rethink their strategies to better leverage the need for consumer knowledge and social networking. In his national best seller *The World Is Flat: A Brief History of the Twenty-First Century*, Thomas L. Friedman suggests the world is "flat" in the sense that globalization has leveled the competitive playing fields between industrial and emerging-market countries. I would also add that we are witnessing the flattening of distribution channels, with drugstores selling food, food stores selling apparel, and superstores selling convenience gas services. The flattening of these channels is fuelled by retailers' need to grow market share away from competitors and other industries. The Internet is one of the key factors in this environment of change, as organizations leverage the same technology, irrespective of distance, to accomplish similar tasks.

If the 1990s was the decade of emotional positioning, the 2000s was an era of experiential branding. Consumer need, state research, and ethnography allow us to clearly understand that a brand is part of a greater lifestyle experience, which lives well before and well after the purchase of the product. Marketers were now challenged to create not only a physical brand experience, but also virtual versions as part of the ever-growing Internet community.

Rearview Mirror Gazing

The issues with the approaches of the past two decades stem from the fact that they are viewed using language and methodologies from the past, while consumers are evolving much more quickly and with less predictability. Whereas twenty years ago the definition of a target market was based on demographics and psychographics, these criteria are no longer effective at capturing the opportunities in the marketplace. We are no longer a group of statistics driven by our age or the type of work we do. The Internet has demonstrated that the marketplace and humanity at large are much more complex. The rapid growth of blogs and online forums has demonstrated that people will enter into new types of relationships that reflect their lifestyle and knowledge needs.

We are entering a new decade where the thought process for how we create experiential brands will need to evolve into creating Belonging Experiences that allow consumers to view brands as a mirror of their lifestyle values. This new way of thinking will help marketers clarify the importance of being a viable channel to the customer while providing value and addressing a heightened consumer need of belonging as part of a community of like-minded citizens.

Social Networks—A Growing Community

Social networks, such as Facebook, YouTube, and LinkedIn, did not exist ten years ago and now account for more readership than some of the best magazine publications. Facebook users, for example, have grown by nearly 300 percent to 18.5 million since last July. Facebook users have uploaded over one billion photos to the Facebook site, and half of those users log in every day, making Facebook about eight times better read than the *New York Times*. These virtual social networks have allowed consumers to have their five minutes of fame on a global basis. Social networks also create a platform to effectively communicate disdain and anger in response to the conduct and claims of organizations. Consumers responding through their social networks wish to demonstrate that they are in a position of control. This has forced organizations to rethink their core values and to ensure transparency in how they approach the market and operate their businesses.

IMPORTANCE OF PLACE

One could believe that with the growth of these virtual networks, the need to have a "branded space" is becoming less important. The reality, however, is very different, since consumers are looking for physical spaces to entertain them: places that offer uniqueness, discovery, trying out, hanging out, empathy, and even transformation. The Trendwatching list of the top ten trends in 2007 included "Being Spaces," public spaces that are there to facilitate out-of-home, out-of-office activities, like watching movies, reading books, meeting friends and colleagues, and so on. I believe that the need for physical contact will grow to counterbalance the virtual world networks.

Although the trend will continue for "Being Spaces" based on consumers' need to network and to be identified as individuals, I believe that these spaces will evolve to Belonging Experiences. These experiences will not only provide a platform to connect with friends, but also become part of a community of like-minded individuals who seek to not only share their stories and experiences, but also provide advice, understanding, and help to the greater community as part of an engaged relationship. I recently visited an ING Café location in the heart of Chicago where such relationships were being created and fostered. People had visited this financial institution not for the basic need to access money, but for a place for them to meet friends and take a break from the hectic pace of work, or just sit around and browse the Web to enrich their knowledge. ING staff were available for conventional banking needs, but they also offered seminars on the most critical needs of young adults entering their wealth-accumulation years.

NEW LEVELS OF INTIMACY

In his book *Living Brands*, Raymond A. Nadeau identified that consumers now demand far more personal contact from highly emotionalized, living brands. He identifies that marketers will need to develop new levels of personal intimacy between brands and their customers. A recent study conducted by the STW Communications Group supports this premise, with 81 percent of those surveyed believing that the feeling of belonging to a community was important and 71 percent believing close communities were lacking in today's society. Brands, such as Starbucks, Second Cup, and Barnes & Noble, continue to demonstrate that brand loyalty is not about selling a better product, but creating a consumer physical experience that answers a deep-rooted human need for belonging and acknowledgment.

Ray Oldenburg is an urban sociologist from Florida who writes about the importance of informal public gathering places. In his book *The Great Good Place*, Oldenburg demonstrates why these gathering places are essential to community and public life. He argues that bars, coffee shops, general stores, and other "third places" (in contrast to the first and second places of home and work) are central to local democracy and community vitality. By exploring how these places work and what roles they serve, Oldenburg supports the premise of the need for consumers to belong and offers tools and insight for individuals and communities everywhere that are applicable to organizations wanting to build strong branded communities. The opportunity exists for organizations to gain understanding of these important factors in creating communities and apply this learning to utilize their physical presence as a key element in forming engaged communities that support their products or services.

CHAPTER TWO
KEY FACTORS DRIVING THE TRENDS

There are millions of trends being tracked by a wide range of researchers, marketers, and brand consultants. Individuals, such as Faith Popcorn, and organizations, such as Trendwatching, GDR Creative Intelligence, and Sputnik, among others, are identifying and keeping tabs on a wide range of trends impacting marketers. In an effort to create understanding as to how consumers interact with brands, I have identified five key factors that support underlying megatrends that lay the foundation for comprehending why creating Belonging Experiences is critical to an organization's success:

- Factor One: Empowered Knowledge
- Factor Two: Belonging Doorways
- Factor Three: Adult Recess
- Factor Four: Experiential Lifestyle
- Factor Five: Vigilant Network

By gaining a better understanding of these five factors and the needs that drive them, we can build a framework for understanding the importance of building Belonging Experiences.

FACTOR ONE: EMPOWERED KNOWLEDGE

Empowered knowledge is fueled by easy access to the Internet, with more than 1 billion consumers online today. Consumers have access to an overwhelming amount of information, with more than 100 billion public Web pages and over 50 million blogs (1.5 million of which are new blogs being posted daily). This factor is driven by consumers' need to be in control and have a clear understanding in order to make the right choices in their lives. Empowered knowledge is as much about learning as sharing information so that others can benefit from the good, the bad, and the ugly experiences.

In the book *2020 Vision*, Davis and Davidson redefine the 80/20 rule. The book notes that by 2020, 80 percent of business profits and market values will come from that part of the enterprise that is built around info business. The new info business will include services that provide turbocharged information, industry-wide product offerings, preview, twenty-four-hour access, and self-design features. IBM and other technology companies have been able to predict the move from product-centric sales to knowledge-based relationships. In 2001, IBM sold its computer manufacturing business to Lenovo so that it could focus its attention on its IT and software business that was generating half the sales but more than 90 percent of the profits. Catherine Fake—one of the cofounders of Flickr, an online image sharing site—responded to a query about why Flickr should not pay to feature traffic-building images posted by consumers, indicating that money was not the key driver for user loyalty. Catherine notes "the ability of connecting with other people, creating an online identity, expressing oneself and not least, garnering other people's attention were more important than being paid to post the images."

Another dimension of the rise of knowledge as currency is the growth of crowd clout to create content and knowledge, such as the rapid acceptance of Wikipedia as a credible new information forum. Don Tapscott supports the point in his book *Wikipedia*, which identifies that the new Web challenges the assumptions that information must move from credentialed producers to passive consumers. Tapscott notes that cocreating with customers is like tapping the most uniquely qualified pool of intellectual capital ever assembled, a pool of talent that is as keenly and uniquely enthusiastic about creating a greater product or service as companies are. Organizations, such as Linux and Wikipedia, were all born from the new business model and consumer need.

The other dimension of this factor is the need for consumers to be empowered to get the most out of life. Abraham Maslow identifies that the highest level of human need is self-actualization, which is articulated by the need to increase our intelligence and thereby chase knowledge. The Web allows for ease of access to information and the sharing of knowledge on a global basis, in real time and evolving daily. Based on the old saying "A little knowledge is a dangerous thing," the new saying centered on today's trends would say, "A lot of knowledge is deadly," since consumers now have the ability to become experts in the most minuscule parts of life.

Although the growth of online knowledge is not anchored in bricks and mortar, it is important to understand that the Web is a tool for retailers and service providers to create ongoing dialogue and collaboration with their customers, allowing their understanding and knowledge learned from other industries and rivals to harness stronger value for the organization. New, inexpensive consumer research tools, such as SurveyMonkey and company blogs, have allowed organizations to seek input and advice, if there is not a clear line to what is driving customer preferences at an extremely affordable cost. Where research and consumer insights used to be the domain of researchers and strategists, companies today are leveraging access to consumer input as part of their performance dashboards and company governance. The ability to engage input from customers at all levels of the organization is one of the pillars of the Belonging Experience model that in turn allows your most loyal customers to promote your offerings as part of a virtual community.

FACTOR TWO: BELONGING DOORWAYS

Maslow's hierarchy of consumer needs is often depicted as a pyramid consisting of five levels. The four lower levels are grouped together and associated with physiological needs, while the top level is termed "Growth Needs." In reviewing Maslow's theory, it is important to note that the need for belonging is truly the doorway between basic physiological and safety needs (the first two levels) and those that are much more aspirational, such as the need for esteem and self-actualization (the last two levels). The "Doorway" is also a metaphor for how the experience fosters an environment where consumers can gain the high level of esteem and self-actualization they seek.

The "Belonging" levels give consumers permission to explore more aspirational needs since their basic needs have been met. Maslow identifies that humans need to feel a sense of belonging and acceptance, whether it comes from large social groups, such as clubs, office culture, and religious groups, or small social connections, such as family and friends. It is important to note the need for belonging can often overcome physiological and security needs. The belonging needs give permission for the growth needs that are identified as the final level in the pyramid, those of cognitive, aesthetic, and self-actualization.

In the *Handbook of Cultural Psychology* by S. Kitayama and D. Cohen (eds.), social relationships are defined as the primary channel through which cultures are transmitted and, conversely, culture informs social relationships. The need for relationships is a foundation to how we learn, through stories and experiences shared by others. Today, these experiences can be shared with thousands of people via the various electronic social networks that allow like-minded people who share similar passions to trade knowledge and information. This occurs because organisms acquire culture by interacting within a social network. Humans have a deep desire and strong drive for wanting to learn from others, including a built-in capacity for imitating learned behaviors. The book identifies that humans also have an ability to modify their behaviors in order to fit within their desired communities. Kitayama and Cohen assert that culture is transmitted through informed social relationships, and knowledge and the ability to self-actualize are predicated by how we integrate our beliefs as part of a social network or community. Social networking sites, such as LinkedIn, Facebook, MySpace, and Twitter, are opening the doorway to shared knowledge and acquired learning.

Another factor impacting the need for belonging is the shift of the family structure. Nearly 10 million Americans 65 years and older, or 30 percent of all noninstitutionalized older persons, live alone (per the 1995 U.S. Bureau of the Census, from the Administration on Aging). In the United States, 34 million people are age 65 and over, representing about one in every eight Americans. Since 1900, the percentage of Americans 65+ has more than tripled, and the number has increased nearly 11 times. Even more dramatic, the 75–84 age-group (11.4 million) was 16 times larger (than in 1900) and the 85+ group (3.8 million) was 31 times larger (U.S. Census Bureau). In addition, over the past 35 years, the proportion of U.S. children being raised in two-parent homes has dropped significantly, from about 85 percent in 1968 to 70 percent in 2003, while the proportion of children living in single-parent homes has nearly doubled. The new family structure is changing the definition of community as social groups, both virtual and tangible are replacing its importance.

FACTOR THREE: ADULT RECESS

"Adult Recess" builds on the need for consumers to take a break from their hectic lives, either as a moment of rejuvenation or a period of stimulation. For many, adult recess is taking that fifteen-minute coffee break in their favorite café, shopping in a mall to discover new items to buy, or just sitting in a bookstore to enjoy mental stimulation. For others, it's visiting an amusement park, rock climbing, or a twenty-minute workout. For this factor, the physical place plays a critical role in answering the consumer need. The current multitasking lifestyle and the growing number of female professionals in the workforce have fueled the need for adult recess. Women comprise just over 50 percent of the U.S. population and make over 80 percent of the consumer purchasing decision.

With the downsizing of America and the constant need to gain efficiencies in manufacturing and operations, consumers today are challenged to fit a thirty-six-hour day into twenty-four. Long gone are the leisurely luncheons and the long afternoon breaks. Recent studies have identified that consumers are working longer and harder than their predecessors. In an era where technology was going to give humans more time to enjoy life, our dependency on our BlackBerries and networked technologies have made us accountable 24/7. Based on a national U.S. study conducted by the National Centre for Chronic Disease Prevention and Health Promotion that tracked trends of physical inactivity from 1994 to 2004, the prevalence of leisure-time physical activity declined significantly, from 29.8 percent in 1994 to 23.7 percent in 2004.

A recent U.S. study by the Federal Reserve Bank of Boston over five decades used surveys to document trends in the allocation of time. The study identified a dramatic increase in leisure time lies behind the relatively stable number of market hours worked (per working-age adult) between 1965 and 2003. Specifically, leisure for men increased by sixty-eight hours per week (driven by a decline in market work hours) and for women by forty-eight hours per week (driven by a decline in home production work hours). This increase in leisure corresponds to roughly an additional five to ten weeks of vacation per year, assuming a forty-hour workweek. The study also found that leisure increased during the last forty years for a number of subsamples of the population, with less educated adults experiencing the largest increases.

Virtual recess is another trend to consider where consumers can create new communities in second-life worlds. By the end of 2011, 80 percent of active Internet users (and *Fortune 500* enterprises) will have a "second life," but not necessarily in the Second Life platform with the creation of avatars as part of software online programs, according to Gartner, Inc. Gartner analysts examined the hype and reality around virtual worlds during Gartner Symposium/ITxpo 2007. Gartner's advice to enterprise clients is that this is a trend that they should investigate and experiment with, but limit substantial financial investments until the environments stabilize and mature. The gaming industry has leveraged this consumer need to connect to virtual communities by developing game systems that allow players from around the world to compete in games ranging from car chases to war games, all from the comfort of their own sofa.

The implication to marketers is that consumers are looking for places to refuel, reenergize, relearn, relax, and very importantly reconnect. As the virtual world continues to play an important role in how much time is allocated to adult recess, place brands will need to step up their presence and value if they do not want to be left out of the race to meet consumers' need for belonging.

FACTOR FOUR: EXPERIENTIAL LIFESTYLE

The need for status remains a key factor in how consumers view brands. A recent Trendwatching report identified that today's consumers are maturing and are increasingly dominated by physical abundance, virtual worlds, individualism, and feelings of guilt and concern about the side effects of unbridled consumption. This has caused a change to what constitutes status, shifting from physical objects to experiences and relationships. Marketers have responded to the understanding that lifestyle needs play an important role by increasing their usage of, and spending on, experiential marketing during 2008, according to a survey of marketers in the United States, the UK, Europe, China, and Australia conducted by Jack Morton Worldwide. The study highlights that 93 percent of respondents agreed that experiential marketing generates advocacy and word-of-mouth recommendations, while 92 percent agreed that experiential marketing builds brand awareness and brand relationships, and 77 percent agreed that it generates sales and leads. Consumer interest in novelty and change has reached its highest level in five years. Not only do consumers want new experiences, but they are also willing to pay more for experiences that are unique and play to their need for fantasy. This need to experiment is driven by the fact that leisure time is becoming increasingly important to consumers, if only because people are living in a society in which employment responsibilities leave little time for genuine relaxation.

In addition, many people today have high levels of personal disposable income (PDI), and falling birth rates also mean that middle-aged consumers have more money to dedicate to the leisure interests of fewer children. Another factor that reinforces the concept of belonging is the emergence of status lifestyles identified by Trendwatching. These new consumer status groups (among others) are divided by lifestyle:

- Transient lifestyles: consumers who live a transient lifestyle, free from the hassle of ownership
- Participative lifestyle: especially for younger consumers where status comes from finding an appreciative audience

- Connecting lifestyles: it's all about who wants to connect to you and how big your network is
- Eco-lifestyle: consumers who are dedicated to sustainable design and living

In his book *Advertising to Baby Boomers*, Chuck Nyren also suggests that boomers are less likely to buy packaged cruises and vacation deals and more likely to want to plan their own experiential travel, relying on the Internet to do it. However, it's important to understand that the definition of experiential travel will vary depending on the baby boomer segment. There are the adventurous travelers who have "been there, done that" and are looking for new experiences, and then there are also the more conservative, less-traveled group that defines adventure as something more low-key, where the relaxation is linked to having someone else take care of all of the details.

The implications to marketers and service providers are significant since they are competing with the experiential need for customers, and the benchmark is being raised for what constitutes an appropriate experience. In addition, the search for the journey through online media is as important as the actual activity selected, leading to the premise that information and knowledge are critical in setting the boundaries for the right experience.

FACTOR FIVE: VIGILANT NETWORK

With the rise of Internet usage by consumers of all ages and a heightened awareness of social and environmental issues, consumers are becoming more vigilant toward how companies operate. With access to social networks, such as YouTube and Facebook (among others), consumers today have an unprecedented platform to blow the whistle on unethical corporate conduct or to demonstrate their support for causes that go beyond the conventional and well-known. This new vigilant network is growing and forcing organizations to rethink their operating and marketing policies. This factor is not limited to only consumers working as part of a network; the market has also responded with the investment community rewarding organizations that are green and committed to sustainability initiatives. This factor is driven by the need for consumers to feel safe and being in control of their lives, not just bystanders as events are shaped. The recent financial downturn, for example, where organizations received government bailout moneys while providing lavish bonuses to their executives, has prompted many blogs and social networks to reprimand their leaders and government officials.

Another trend that falls within this factor is "Crowd Clout," defined by Trendwatching as an online grouping of citizens/consumers for a specific cause, be it political, civic, or commercial, aimed at everything from bringing down politicians to forcing suppliers to fork over discounts. This trend is also the result of consumers' need to be engaged in the creation of products and services. Online buying organizations, such as Priceline.com, or brands, such as Nike and Levi's, have capitalized on this trend by offering either price comparisons when looking for the ideal product or the opportunity to personalize the purchase experience by designing your own style of running shoes or jeans.

With a billion people online and the numbers growing exponentially, consumers are networked beyond geographical boundaries that once dictated style, needs, and social requirements. These consumers are skilled bargain seekers and value hunters. They're savvy online networkers who have been leveraging the Web for half a decade, and they're opinionated reviewers and advisers. This growing network of like-minded consumers will provide no shortage of online content through pictures, movies, and stories, especially with younger generations playing a key role; those Generation X and Y that are born to the Web, to whom contributing online is second nature and an everyday ritual. They will demand transparency of values, beliefs, price, and service from brands and organizations. Those that do not conform to their beliefs or values will be judged and penalized in a matter of minutes, on a global basis.

This huge online audience is also made up of keen shoppers with the most recent U.S. data identifying that $200 billion in sales were conducted online last year. European consumers spent 100 billion euros online buying everything from travel to products and services. A new buying power through a shared network has emerged, shifting the buying power from retailers to social networks. There is a "free" dimension of the vigilant network, with the rise of BitTorrent sites for easy downloading of free music or the emergence of shareware programs, such as Linux. Youth culture has adopted this free culture with gusto, with free stuff perhaps dominating free learning and open source software programs that are free and can be easily enhanced. The trend has already impacted large well-established industries such as the music industry with 20 percent drop in recorded music sales reported by the RIAA in the first quarter of 2007, compared to the first quarter 2006. For the same period, the industry has seen an increase of 35 percent of Internet traffic attributed to bitTorrent packaged media files. The challenge for brands is to remain transparent while evolving their offering beyond commodities to avoid the free attitude of the future generations.

CONNECTING THE DOTS

The factors outlined are based on key megatrends and consumer needs that are currently being channeled to impact everyday lives and highlight the need for a Belonging Experience. Let's look at just a few implications that you can harness within your organization.

Evolve Offering, Restructure Processes

Organizations need to evolve their approach from the transaction-focused aspect of selling products to providing added-value services that are built on the customer's hunger for knowledge and understanding. Financial institutions, investment houses, and some retailers are expanding their loyalty by offering knowledge-based services that clearly tap an unmet consumer need. Which aspect of your organization is focused around knowledge and how you leverage this aspect of your brand to build acquired knowledge amongst customers are becoming the real value.

A great example in the technology retailing industry is the recent acquisition of Geek Squad by Best Buy. The added branded service leverages knowledge of how to set up networks, systems, and IT programs within your house or office. Although Geek Squad does sell products, its true value to consumers is knowledge that has a dollar value equation. IBM is another organization that has evolved to leverage empowered knowledge. The organization clearly identified that the road to success was paved by selling knowledge and not products. IBM identified business performance transformation services, a mix that includes IT and business process outsourcing along with intelligent software and consulting services, representing a $500 billion market that is growing at a significant rate.

Leverage the Experience as a Doorway to Empowering Consumers

Take a look at the current physical manifestation of your brand to identify areas of opportunity where knowledge and understanding are key in transforming consumer needs into aspirational desires. What are the key transactional processes that you need to retain and that can be evolved to take advantage of how consumers seek information? What new aspects of your consumer experience do you need to add to give your organization credibility to sell knowledge? What type of knowledge is the consumer seeking, and how can you best deliver this information within your environment?

We need to think beyond signing and in-store conventional communication, since these tools do not create a changed behavior or effectively communicate new innovative ways to think. The true opportunity is to disrupt the way consumers interact with your brand in order to create a new behavioral platform that will allow for a new understanding and empowering process. We need to think about how the physical aspect translated by all of the senses can play a role in changing behavior and create a doorway to the acceptance and willingness to pay for knowledge. Currently, very few retailers or service organizations have been able to break through to gain ground in this opportunity. Another dimension is the ability of organizations to clearly understand key hidden and stated needs that are currently not being met by competitors. Establishing a better understanding of consumer needs is the surest way of building a strong brand experience and gaining permission to sell knowledge as a value proposition.

HR: A KEY FACTOR FOR CHANGE

A key factor in ensuring the experience delivers on the need for consumers to feel empowered is a rethinking of the role of in-the-trenches staff in building this bridge from the tangible to the intangible. The expression "What gets measured gets done" could not be more applicable to changing established behaviors within organizations. As humans, we are all reluctant to change since it comes with a certain level of risk. Organizations that want to transform their operations into a knowledge-centric, consumer-empowering process will need to reevaluate their hiring, training, and operational practices to determine how the frontline staff can live the new brand promise and experience.

Creating a physical change in the operating environment is just one of the steps required to make the transformation a success. Developing clear performance metrics and success criteria that are evaluated on an ongoing basis are additional tools that will be required. The definition of target groups needs to be redefined. In order to build a house on solid foundation, it is important to review current customer target group information in order to better define the profiles based on cognitive, aesthetic, and self-actualization human needs. Through the use of research tools that clearly identify consumers' unmet emotional and rational needs, we can better understand how these can be clustered as part of like-minded communities that share similar lifestyle and culture needs.

My experience has identified that such research and reevaluation of the target groups demonstrate that traditional segmentation such age and gender may not be the only discriminators for how consumers respond to brands. For example, the growth of business ownership by women, the increased prevalence of single-sex relationships, and the growth of importance, awareness, and active participation of consumers in social issues ranging from HIV to climate change has demonstrated that shared values play a critical role in how we view brands and the world.

EXPLORE THE FULL CONSUMER TOUCHPOINT CONTINUUM

The new Belonging Experience occurs well before and well after the actual physical experience occurs. Understanding how you foster a sense of community at all of the consumer touchpoints is critical. In order to draw attention to the fact that your brand experience has changed and the offering has evolved beyond transactional services or discounted products, you will need to disrupt current perceptions of your organization at every contact point.

The use of an integrated communication program that talks to the hidden needs of customers in a way that disrupts their current thinking is a very effective tool. A recent Scotiabank campaign, "You're richer than you think" has been very effective in getting customers to think differently about their conventional bank transactions. It sets up the financial institution in a different light, which reinforces the need for understanding and knowledge.

CHAPTER THREE
BRAND ENGAGEMENT

The word "engagement" defines the action of being committed, of occupying a presence, or of attracting or causing someone to become involved. For marketers, the word clearly defines the level of brand loyalty and repeat purchase, the true measures of the health of a brand. The challenge for marketers is to define the most effective approach in engaging their target group within an environment where consumers are being bombarded with a wide range of messages and offers from a broad source of vehicles. Today, consumers lack the time to explore the right option to suit their needs or the level of risk to try something new. Adding to the challenge, customers and employees are skeptical about company claims and commitments, and they are confused about who is working in their best interest. The market downturn and the erosion of corporate credibility have further fueled this sense of confusion.

This chapter will identify the three critical sides of engagement and the needs driving each side of the pyramid, while providing an approach on how to increase the level of brand loyalty for your organization.

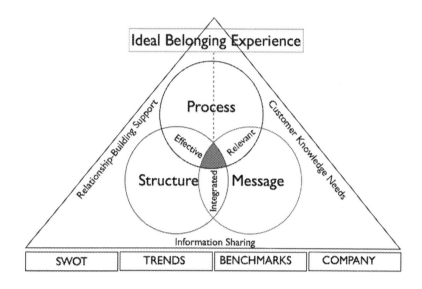

Exhibit 1: Engagement Triangle

Each of these three dimensions (Exhibit 1) plays a critical role in building engagement with customers and ensuring strong brand loyalty. Each dimension of the Engagement Triangle builds on the Belonging Experiences model, supporting a strong understanding that there are numerous factors that come to play in ensuring customers are truly engaged in brands. A recent Forrester study on the influence of brand experience on brand loyalty clearly identifies a direct correlation between the overall experience in which consumers engage with brands and the level of commitment toward purchasing additional products or the reluctance of switching to competitive brands.

Organizations that have defined the key elements to engaging the consumer as part of a unique and well-defined experience in a way that is relevant and meaningful have been able to gain significant market share and brand loyalty. In addition, understanding the role of the various marketing tools and messages as part of each of the different consumer touchpoints that support an engagement process will help ensure strong long-term relationships. The Engagement Pyramid also helps define the role that the different moments of truth and the employees play in its success.

WHY IS ENGAGEMENT SO IMPORTANT?

In December 2006 and January 2007, the Economist Intelligence Unit, a division of *The Economist* business magazine, conducted an online study with 311 executives on their companies' customer engagement practices. The respondents covered the globe with approximately 32 percent of respondents from Western and Eastern Europe, 32 percent from the Americas, 31 percent from the Asia-Pacific region, and 5 percent from other parts of the world. Respondents represented a wide range of industries, functions, and revenue levels. The survey indicated that executives in a variety of industries believe customer engagement moves beyond customer loyalty and satisfaction to provide a crucial competitive advantage. As markets become commodities through aggressive competition and the flattening of the innovation process, companies have identified a need to evolve beyond the conventional marketing initiatives to better engage their most valued customers.

The research findings identified that, despite their general optimism and strong understanding about the value of customer engagement programs and strategies, many respondents identified that they find them difficult to implement in their own companies. The study supports my belief that what is lacking within the industry is a process that allows organizations to foster new and unique engagement strategies. The study outlined a list of strategies that included cultivating a closer understanding of the customer and what he or she expects from the company in order to become more fully committed. The study clearly identified the need to translate the voice of the consumer into engagement opportunities while clearly defining customer segments. The study also supports the Engagement Pyramid model since it takes into consideration the role of technology in creating engagement and identifies how new technologies can help to engage customers.

The findings are further supported by a Gallup Consulting Group 2008 study on why banks must carefully manage their digital touchpoints to create a seamless customer experience. The study was launched to investigate the role interactive technology plays in creating engagement among retail banking customers. Gallup Consulting conducted a survey of more than 2,100 people in six countries. The survey found that extremely satisfied Web site users are seven times more likely to be engaged with their bank when compared to less satisfied Web site users. Extremely satisfied mobile banking users are fifteen times more likely to be engaged with their bank when compared to less satisfied mobile banking users.

Customers tend to be more engaged with their bank when they use many of their bank's Web site features, use certain features that have an especially strong connection with engagement, and/ or interact with their bank across many different touchpoints (both digital and nondigital). In most cases the overall level of engagement of customers who use their bank's Web site is not substantially different from the engagement of those who do not. However, customer satisfaction with a bank's Web site is strongly related to overall engagement with the bank. More than half of the retail banking customers in many countries visit their bank's Web site, and approximately one in ten use a mobile device to conduct transactions with their bank. The Gallup study also identified four types of engagement that were based on the combination of attitudinal loyalty and emotional attributes:

- Fully engaged: loyal and strongly attached
- Engaged: less strongly connected, with somewhat lower attachment and loyalty
- Not engaged: emotionally and attitudinally neutral, no emotional connection

- Actively disengaged: active emotional detachment and even antagonism to your company

PROCESS: A KEY FACTOR IN IDENTIFYING CUSTOMER KNOWLEDGE NEEDS

Where are all of these insights leading? I believe that today's consumers are not buying products or services; they are seeking knowledge that would allow them to make the right decision on their quest to get their given job completed. In his blog *Experiencematters.com*, Bruce Temkin, a senior researcher for Forrester, identified six laws of customer experience. One of these laws identifies that every interaction creates a personal reaction, where the individual needs of customers must be taken into consideration and prioritized by customer segments.

The beginning of any engaging relationship is established through organizations' ability to guide consumers through the purchase decision by clearly understanding which segment is being served and what tools best meet their given knowledge needs. For example, if you are a packaged goods company, it may be more about how to provide a quick, balanced meal the whole family can enjoy while being healthy. If you are a consumer seeking to buy a house, the need may focus on the knowledge of how to best negotiate a mortgage versus shopping for the best mortgage rate.

The customer's ability to feel empowered and knowledgeable is a critical factor in creating the platform for an engaging experience on the journey to brand loyalty. The process follows similar fundamentals as to how consumers build personal relationships and foster a sense of belonging. Most people do not get married following the first date. By understanding the courtship process and how your brand's touchpoints play an important role in gaining the customer's awareness, interest, and ultimately trust, and how information about your brand is shared, companies create a strong platform for customer loyalty. With the advent of Web

2.0, consumers are connecting with brands and communities at an incredible rate, and the power of a single individual to impact the perception on a massive scale is challenging organizations on the processes they use to get consumers engaged in their brands.

HP, one of the leading technology companies that have embraced the power of Web 2.0 and the new realities of how consumers connect with brands, has noted that there has been a significant shift in advertising dollars to online media. Whereas it took 127 years for newspapers and 25 years for cable television to reach $20 billion in ad revenues in the United States, online media has garnered that amount in just 13 short years. A Booz Allen study conducted in 2008 identified that 90 percent of marketers understand the urgent need to adapt their marketing approach. Four out of five marketers surveyed believe consumer insights are more important than they were five years ago and will be even more important in the future. The process factor in the engagement model identifies different steps that an organization needs to take into consideration when enticing customers into a relationship. Critical questions, such as "When does the customer first identify the given 'job' need?" and "How is this translated in key and hidden drivers?" need to be addressed. Consumers may want to purchase new tires for their car, but what is the true need being fulfilled? Is it performance, or is it a reflection of their self-image as it relates to their car?

The initial stage of the engagement process should provide marketers with the ability to clearly understand the emotive needs of customers. What steps should the company put into place to gain an understanding of the customer's needs? The role of research and customer feedback loops and the point of the relationship at which these should be initiated are all part of the engagement analysis process. More importantly, the key steps customers take on their journey to build relationships with your brand need to be defined by critical moments of truth where your brand needs to deliver on the customers' needs. Understanding how your brand maps across these moments of truth and what job each of these moments needs to accomplish to provide customers with a sense of recognition and control is the first step in building a strong engagement program.

With new RFID and GPS technologies being integrated, firms, such as Google, are redefining consumer living and lifestyle patterns and identifying groups of consumers based on their special behaviors, such as how long they mingle in given areas within a city, how many of them have similar behaviors (tribes), and how these behaviors impact purchase patterns within geographical shopping areas. In the future, these tools will allow marketers to clearly understand how their brands impact geographical and communal behaviors. The message, the approach, and the content all help to effectively connect with customers.

Most successful brands have built their loyalty around a well-devised script, which narrates a brand story that clearly connects on both an emotional and a rational level.

For example, the Mac and Windows computer wars that have raged for the past twenty years between the two platforms have created the opportunity for Apple to create a distinctive story that has effectively connected with its loyal base. In the epic story, the Mac user is trying to overcome uniformity and the fear of a lack of creativity. The Mac-versus-Windows commercials clearly create a story that follows similar scripting found in blockbuster movies. Actors emulate the key characteristics of each brand, with the PC being cleverly portrayed as the villain, while the Mac plays the role of the hero.

Mac users can relate to the commercial, since the script of overcoming the dominance of the Windows platform while wanting a life that provides greater simplicity and creative possibilities clearly resonates with them. Apple has created a story that allows their loyal customers to feel part of a unique tribe of customers who all share similar values. It is mirrored in real-life situations when people meet in social gatherings that share the same Mac platform. The ability of the message to create a strong link between the consumer need and the product offering is critical, while the way in which the content changes based on the different moments of truth ensures the right level of engagement throughout the brand purchase process. By aligning the key message content to the level of engagement by customers, you are ensuring that the right message is being noticed, and that it mirrors the knowledge needs of the customer.

THE STRUCTURE ENSURES THE RIGHT SUPPORT AND ENVIRONMENT TO ENSURE ENGAGEMENT

An organization's ability to reflect on the ideal brand experience while taking into consideration the engagement needs of its customer base is key in gaining consumer commitment to its brand. The need for all aspects of the experience to provide a focused and supported approach is critical in ensuring a strong level of commitment. The structure should reflect the different steps consumers undertake to connect with brands and allocate the right level of service, information, and tools to ensure each given step reflects the needs of the customer. The structure component of the Engagement Pyramid considers the type of engagement, its length, and the desired customer outcome.

The organization's Web presence, available information, telephone service, and opportunity for consumers to connect with a live company representative or an alternative to actually shopping the retail location all play critical roles in how best to structure an engaging relationship.

Another critical structure element is the way the organization supports its frontline associates—those who manage the customer relationship. Julie Moll, senior vice president, and Janet Smalley, vice president, of brand research represented Marriott International during their presentation "Engaging the customer in a changing marketplace." Julie and Janet started their presentation with one simple statement: "Have a vision." Marriott's vision is simple: customer performance, loyalty, and love. Their vision is simply to perform outstandingly well for their customers, develop a sense of loyalty with the customer and associates, and build on a loving relationship that potentially goes beyond the confines of a monetary interaction. The presentation stressed the point that a brand is more than a logo or advertisement—it's a relationship and a promise. The first step in ensuring delivery of a brand promise (and to start building the relationship) is to take care of your associates. It is a simple equation: take care of the associate, the associate takes care of the customer, the customer comes back, and the money takes care of itself. We all know about our target audience, but many forget to target associates.

A J.D. Power study found that overall satisfaction with the retail banking experience has decreased considerably since 2007—down 26 index points on a 1,000-point scale to 737 in 2008. The study also shows that banks that provide high levels of customer satisfaction have more highly committed customers, which is essential to financial growth. In addition, J.D. Power conducted a wireless study that identified that while the average wait time for customers to be greeted after they first enter a wireless store is approximately five minutes, overall satisfaction declines considerably if the wait time exceeds thirty seconds. Currently only 28 percent of respondents cited speaking to a qualified sales representative within one minute of entering a retail store. The quality of sales staff is ranked as the most important aspect across all retail models:

- Importance of sales staff (51 percent)
- Store display (17 percent)
- Store facility (16 percent)
- Price/promotion (16 percent)

If customers are delighted with the sales process, they are seven times more likely to shop the location again for future purchases and nine times more likely to recommend it to a friend. The study supports the importance that each element of the experience be structured in an approach that ensures a positive perception at each brand touchpoint. In one of my white papers, "Not all Moments of Truth are Equal," I identified that organizations need to evaluate each of their moments of truth and establish a structure that eliminates any barrier to creating an engaging relationship. The paper clearly identified that not all moments of truth are equal and, depending on the type of organization (CPG versus service versus retail), these moments of truth may vary in importance and overall impact on the customer experience.

PUTTING THE ENGAGEMENT PYRAMID IN CONTEXT

Successful organizations have leveraged the principles found in the Engagement Pyramid either unknowingly or through consultation with my firm as part of a rebranding exercise. These organizations have realized the importance of leveraging a change in their physical presence and consumer touchpoints as well as a staff behavioral change to better reflect the needs of customers. Through a redesign of their total customer experience—from the way they gain information on the Web to how they change the transaction process to mirror the consumer need for knowledge and understanding—companies have realized this approach is the only means to evolve and provide a strong competitive advantage. The Engagement Pyramid is a model that allows better alignment with how consumers want to be treated and interact with brands. More importantly, the model gives organizations the appropriate tools to reinvent themselves by guiding them through the reengineering process, ensuring that all aspects of the experience—from the Web to the actual transaction process— reflect the "job" needs of customers.

Umpqua Bank, Redefining Engagement

Umpqua is a leading regional bank on the U.S. West Coast that has built a reputation on fostering an engagement experience. The financial institution was ranked the thirteenth best company to work for in the United States by *Fortune Magazine* and boasts a community program (with 147 branches and its own coffee blend) giving employees forty hours of paid time each year to volunteer in the community. Umpqua Bank started with only six employees in Canyonville, Oregon, in 1953. Umpqua's number-one goal isn't to be the biggest bank in the world; it's to deliver the best banking experience possible.

One of the ways they are achieving this is by remaining tightly tied to the communities served by the bank. By contributing staff time and resources to local organizations and events, Umpqua makes a difference in the communities they live and work in. Umpqua has a deep-rooted belief that when the community succeeds, they all succeed.

When it comes to banking, Umpqua has put great emphasis on creating new experiences for their customers to enjoy. Although the experience is about all facets of banking, Umpqua's focus has been on exceeding its customers' expectations. That's why, in addition to taking care of transactions, Umpqua offers its own blend of coffee, a computer café, and local music. Many of their stores even offer after-hours activities, from financial seminars to knitting and book clubs. Umpqua firmly believes the more enjoyable banking is, the less it will feel like an errand. Since the philosophy needed to be reflected in the moments of truth translated as part of the physical assets of the branch, an innovative experience was created. Umpqua associates experience an empowering environment full of opportunities for rewards, recognition, professional growth, and valuable time toward an industry-leading, employer-paid volunteer program. In fact, it was its associates who voted Umpqua Bank among *Oregon Business*

Magazine's "100 Best Companies to Work For" ten times since 1996, taking it to the top of the list in 2004.

Umpqua embodies the principles of the Engagement Pyramid, since the leadership of the organization has reviewed their entire customer experience to better reflect their needs and become a pillar in the community that has gone well beyond banking. The organization reassessed its processes to better reflect a community atmosphere that mirrors similar behaviors found in local cafés where people can read, relax, and enjoy a great cup of coffee. Umpqua also understood the customers' job of gaining better knowledge of their financial options through the use of in-branch seminars and workshops, in addition to the need to socialize and create a strong sense of belonging to the community. The process also goes against the conventional thinking of some banks that discourage customers from entering a bank branch and other banks that compete against the Internet to provide convenience and speed. Conversely, Umpqua's new store inspires and encourages its customers to relax and take their time when making financial decisions. Guided by Zibra, the design firm responsible for the new direction, they redefined the meaning of the branch, renaming the experience "Greenspace." The new bank store is more than an environment; it's an experience. Shopping modules encourage customers to buy gift cards and open green-friendly or business accounts. The message to customers and the community also reflected the new position. Signing and staff engagement processes were reevaluated, and merchandising tables were incorporated to promote special programs and keep the bank fresh and relevant. Customers are encouraged to browse the aisles, allowing Umpqua's Universal Associates to approach them in a nonthreatening, conversational way. The shopping experience encourages customers to think and act on their financial future. The structure—from the staff training, IT infrastructure, and branch policies and operations—supports the friendly and caring position of the bank. From the vision of the CEO to the level of understanding and role of engagement of the frontline staff, the entire organization was realigned to a common vision and focus.

GRAND & TOY: REDEFINING SMALL-BUSINESS ENGAGEMENT

Grand & Toy, Canada's largest commercial office products company and a division of OfficeMax, was looking to reposition the company and evolve the thinking to better reflect the needs of its small-business customers who are looking for more than just conventional supplies. Rather than match the big box stores in terms of volume or variety, G&T chose instead to focus on exclusive, quality products and specialized office services that catered to the customer segment needs. The G&T organization wanted a new experience that clearly engaged the small home and office entrepreneurs, offering them a place that understood and accommodated their specific needs. They developed a new experience to capitalize on the need for small-business owners to feel empowered and as mighty as the big companies with whom they competed. A Belonging Experience process was initiated that incorporated the Engagement Pyramid model to assist in Grand & Toy's business transformation as part of a new "store of the future" design. The challenge was to fit the new design within the existing space while maximizing the merchandise mix and assortment, which had been reduced to provide areas for new services.

A second and more critical challenge was the need to persuade customers into using the new consultative services that formed the foundation of the new concept. G&T had built its business by providing companies with business-to-business sales and office supplies while leveraging its retail presence to reinforce the brand's offering. The engagement challenge was to change the behavior of current and new customers without alienating existing shoppers.

The structure had to change if the concept was going to effectively engage customers. Shikatani Lacroix (SL), the design firm responsible for the new direction, developed a new store environment that clearly promoted the added-value knowledge and service areas, from the designer work area and small-business consultation offices to the new technology demonstration area. All facets were developed to leverage the sharing of knowledge. SL designed the space using high-end features that are rooted in functionality. Curved linear design and custom millwork were applied to the key service stations that act as customer interaction zones. Custom display features were installed with unique color treatments to provide a clean, uncomplicated backdrop for the products and keep surfaces free from clutter.

The new store included a flex area supported by digital technology that allowed for the use of workshops and seminars. This gave small-business owners the opportunity to expand their knowledge of the newest technologies and business approaches. Special consultation offices were also created to provide small-business owners with access to knowledgeable business consultants who could assist in everything from setting up a business and managing the payroll to setting up the best IT infrastructure to meet small-business needs. Comfortable seating was located outside the offices to provide a relaxing place to read the latest in business information while waiting for a meeting. As part of the messaging facet, a signage package was also developed providing an optimal level of communication while remaining relatively simple in execution and presentation. It was very important that from the exterior of the store, customers clearly understood the new offerings and services being provided.

The intention was to provide key customer touchpoints throughout the store to emphasize the idea of Grand & Toy as a unique retail experience and a partner to small businesses. Both clients and customers have described the overall effect as more intimate and very welcoming. G&T supported the entire customer experience with a new staff-training program that was both Internet- and one-on-one–based. The organization understood the importance of modifying the staff behavior to evolve the engagement process. This new behavior would reflect the new key moments of truth that form the new experience. Everything from the advertising, the Web site, and the store experience allowed the staff to engage the customers and change their understanding of what G&T could provide them. The store focal points allowed staff to better engage customers on the new services that were based on allowing small-business owners to effectively compete and succeed in the marketplace.

NIKE GOES BEYOND PRODUCTS TO ENGAGE CUSTOMERS INTO FITNESS MOMENTS

To create a strong engagement experience, you do not necessarily need to be a retailer. Leading sports shoe marketer Nike recently leveraged the power of engaging its customers in order to protect its market share. In partnership with Apple, the Nike+ program links the sports shoe to a fitness management program that is supported by a Web site. With the launch of this program, Nike has redefined engagement and brand loyalty. The Nike+ product will only work as part of a Web site, allowing users to download their performance and develop new programs. The use of an online program reinforces the sense of a unique community, where information related to the individual's unique needs is captured and managed. Based on its success with iTunes, Apple already had that knowledge and forged a partnership with Nike to expand its dominance of the music network while furthering the use of the iPod. Sales of the iPod Nano have been stellar since the introduction of the new program, and this partnership is just one more way that Apple is extending its reach. It's no surprise that one of the key supports in running is music, which Apple delivers so brilliantly. Apple worked with Nike to create a user interface and program that is easy to use and intuitive to how runners program their activities.

This kit not only is tied to the Nike+ Web site, but Apple is also taking advantage of the engagement level, by allowing individuals to form running communities and providing a forum for them to connect with like-minded runners within their neighborhood. Some of the workouts feature Nike coaches, like Alberto Salazar (multiple-marathon champion), giving encouragement and instruction on ways to improve endurance, while others are music playlists developed solely with the runner in mind by the likes of Crystal Method and LCD Soundsystem. The success of the Nike+ program supports the Engagement Pyramid concept by clearly understanding the "job" requirements of its target group and redefining a process and structure that answers its specific needs. The combination of a new process, a key message of customization and community, and a structure aligned with Apple has allowed Nike to create a new brand experience that clearly differentiates its products from any of its competitors.

DOVE: REDEFINING A SENSE OF COMMUNITY ENGAGEMENT

The Dove Campaign for Real Beauty, supported by the Self-Esteem Fund, is another great example of a brand creating an engaging experience. Dove, Unilever's leading soap brand, clearly understood that their product was providing far greater benefits than just cleaning the body. Dove's research identified the need for women to build their self-esteem, which has been shaken and distorted by the media's promotion of perfect bodies to sell products.

The engagement experience begins with a Web site that clearly communicates the self-esteem proposition, which is supported by tools, workshops, and videos. The goal of the site is to build an engaging network that can support the overall vision by hosting self-esteem workshops in the consumers' communities. The site provides great motivational information and tools to help women clearly understand how the media and the importance of celebrating their individuality have stereotyped them. The Dove story clearly supports the foundation of the Engagement Pyramid with the use of the Dove Self-Esteem Fund to clearly establish a set of behaviors different from the branded side of the business. The advertising clearly reinforces the self-esteem message and drives the audience to an online community where more information and tools are provided.

The success is derived through a single-minded and focused approach, with all aspects of the various moments of truth aligned to support the vision. As part of the structure, Dove allows access to mentors and mothers, or it enlists the support of women who want to take up the cause by becoming coaches and hosting seminars within their communities. The engagement process succeeds since Dove has clearly identified the hidden need of female consumers to feel special and valued. Dove also supports the belief that you do not need to be a retailer to provide an engaging experience.

PUTTING THE ENGAGEMENT PYRAMID TO WORK

The previous pages have outlined the fundamentals of the Engagement Pyramid, the reasons it is important to ensure your organization has an engagement strategy, and examples of organizations that have embraced the principles. The challenge is putting the learning into action in order for you to leverage an engaging experience for your brand. A study conducted by *The Economist* clearly identified that the missing link between the need and the effective execution is the lack of an effective process. I have outlined in this section the potential steps you can utilize to build stronger brand loyalty and customer commitment.

Step One: Understanding the Voice of the Consumer (VOC) and Employee (VOE)

All engagement initiatives start and end with the customer. What many organizations fail to understand is the need to also factor in the voice of the employees. Understanding their needs and level of commitment to the engagement process will ensure the creation of a stronger focused effort. Without a strong link between both the needs of the consumer and those of the employees, most engagement programs fail. The initial step in leveraging the engagement process is to clearly understand the individual and unique needs of customers, from both an emotional and rational dimension. Understanding how these needs may vary pending socio-demographic factors and lifestyle needs as part of a "voice of the customer" (VOC). The use of quantitative study to identify these segments will ensure the right process, message, and structures are put into place. It is also important that while organizations develop a strong understanding of the VOC, they clearly understand the needs, motivations, and beliefs of their staff that will in the future support the new engagement model. An employee study should clearly identify where the organization is aligned in comparison with the VOC and where gaps exist that will need to be filled in order to support the effective implementation and management of the engagement process. The key insights regarding both the VOC and VOE will serve as the platform for redefining the ideal engagement process.

Step Two: Identifying the Ideal Value Proposition

Based on the key learning from the VOC and VOE research, it is critical that an evaluation of the current and future value proposition for your organization or brand be initiated. The value proposition needs to take into account the functional, emotional, and cognitive needs of the most loyal customers while also considering the needs of employees. What is the true cost to the customer for buying your brand? How are the brand's key benefits bringing value to overcome the cost, and how much of the brand's value is derived from tangible versus intangible benefits? All of these questions need to be answered to clearly understand how a value proposition can bring meaning to engaging consumers and build stronger brand loyalty.

The value proposition exercise needs to be effectively translated back to the VOC and VOE in a way that is meaningful and relevant to their needs. With a clearly articulated value proposition, the organization has the right bearing on the compass to start navigating a new engagement journey that will result in stronger brand loyalty.

STEP THREE: DEFINING THE LEARNING RACE ANALYSIS

The RACE acronym is the filter to use when evaluating any engagement opportunity: repurpose/reduce, align/add, consolidate/communicate, and eliminate. These four key factors should be leveraged when exploring your current brand offering and how you can transform it into a more engaging experience. In order to successfully do so, it is important to consider the advent of current and emerging technologies. A decade ago, for example, customers did not have the same access to knowledge and purchase opportunities on the Internet. Today, however, it is the primary tool used by millions to make the right buying decisions, and it plays a critical role in how people engage with organizations and brands. The ultimate outcome of the first step in the RACE process is to clearly identify where the organization is today and where it needs to evolve in the future to better align with customers.

- **R**epurpose/Reduce: Review the current moments of truth for your brand and determine which of these moments needs to be repurposed or reduced to provide a stronger engagement with customers. It could be the amount of literature that you are offering or the number of messages you are promoting that needs to be reconsidered. Based on the VOC and VOE, develop a clear understanding of what process, message, or structures are not bringing any value to the engagement process. Through this exercise, you will discover facets of your go-to-market strategies that actually create confusion and clutter and get in the way of effectively connecting your brand with customers.

- **A**lign/Add: As you review your operation, you need to determine how your current processes, messaging, and structures align with the key moments of truth for each of your customer segments. Weed out processes or structures that do not align with how consumers want to engage with your brand, and identify those that currently do not exist within your organization that will need to be added to align effectively with the needs of each of your core customer segments.

- **C**onsolidate/Communicate: As you create the ideal engagement model for your organization, it is important to determine if there are efficiencies that can be derived from consolidating some of your processes, messaging, and structures. If the Internet is the most effective tool in the initial stages of empowering your target group, what should you communicate on your Web site, and what process should be consolidated as part of this information platform? With the advent of digital signing and communication, what is the ideal approach in leveraging this new technology in communicating to customers? Are digital posters the answer, or should they evolve to become media-rich content that will energize your target group to take action? A thorough review of how you communicate with your customers at each of the consumer touchpoints needs to be implemented in order to determine which should be consolidated to become more effective.

- **E**liminate: Of the four letters, this step demands the most scrutiny and education. The key challenge is deciding which part of the current processes, messaging, and structures needs to be eliminated to give way to more effective engagement approaches. The difficulty in eliminating current approaches is not the ability to identify them, but more importantly, the process required to convince the organization that these elements have become legacies of the past that do not bring any value to the engagement process. It may require an effective education process to gain the organization's support on the need to eliminate certain processes and approaches since some of these may reside in divisions that have ultimate decision power over their use. It may also require a stringent internal communication and education program that will gain alignment with the key insights and need for change throughout the development phases of a new or modified engagement strategy.

STEP FOUR: ALIGNING THE ORGANIZATION WITH THE NEW ENGAGEMENT MODEL

Once you have a strong understanding of the various Engagement Pyramid elements that need to evolve, it is important to ensure that the organization properly supports the new process. All facets of the company need to be considered, from HR and IT to marketing, sales, research and development, and operations. Each division of the organization needs to clearly embrace the new engagement model while setting specific strategies and action plans that will support the transition from the old model to the new. This becomes more critical if the RACE analysis identified significant changes to the current business model. A key factor in ensuring support is the development of a leadership team that has a strong, visible endorsement from senior management. This will allow the organization to balance priorities and ensure the right resources are allocated to the new initiative.

Another factor, which should be considered to ensure success, is the development of clearly articulated metrics for the new engagement process. These metrics would take into consideration both the quantifiable and intangible facets of performance. Market share, mind share, frequency of purchase, percentage of sales that are not on promotion, depth of relationship with customers, length of relationship, perceptions, and attitudes toward the company would all form metrics that should be tracked throughout the test stages.

Finally, creating a strong internal communication and learning platform will ensure a higher degree of alignment. The use of symbols and statements, in addition to mission statements that are easy to understand and translate into action, would form part of the ongoing support that will help the organization put the new initiatives into focus. It is critical for any new engagement process to be fully embraced by the organization at all levels. A key component of this support is the ability of the organization to get its employees on board while clearly identifying the desired behavior.

STEP FIVE: PROTOTYPING THE ENGAGEMENT MODEL

Building on the organization's alignment and support, I recommend the initiation of a live market test to provide further understanding and to ensure the most effective approach prior to a system-wide launch. Prototyping allows organizations to test different options and approaches within the safe haven of a hypothetical situation to gain the best learning prior to launch. Allowing for a degree of failure will provide a solid platform for the organization to determine the optimum balance between risk and opportunity. It will also provide the leadership team with the opportunity to evaluate the approach and provide recommendations based on the realities of the marketplace. Finally, a prototype will allow the organization to explore how the actual support and frontline staff embrace the new engagement process while identifying additional operational and HR adjustments that would not be possible in a large-scale launch. A test will also ensure that all facets of the engagement process have adequate validation and input prior to a formal implementation.

STEP SIX: CONSTANT EVALUATION AND MONITORING

The ideal engagement model must evolve as the customer needs evolve based on a wide range of factors (i.e., socio-demographic shifts, new technologies, new competitive threats from unrelated industries, a shift in the organization's manufacturing process, etc.). The test phase should lead to a system-wide launch to provide the optimum efficiencies. (Running two separate programs for any length of time is costly and requires significant resources.) The rollout phase should be monitored since it impacts a wide range of the organization's structure and operations. As such, it is important to have constant communication and support throughout the transition phase. By creating an environment that constantly evaluates, adjusts, and modifies its approach, organizations and brands can ensure they remain relevant and meaningful to their core target group. In addition, by evaluating the engagement process, the organization can also identify ongoing efficiencies that could result in higher margins while allowing for a better focus on the key engagement facets that provide the most benefit in the customer relationship.

CHAPTER FOUR
THE CASE FOR BELONGING
EXPERIENCES

John Seely Brown, former chief scientist of Xerox and director emeritus of Xerox Palo Alto Research Center, is well-known for developing innovative processes. His proclamation, "The best way of looking forward is looking around since the future is already here," could not be more applicable to helping define who has already embarked (knowingly or unknowingly) on developing Belonging Experiences. In reviewing the marketplace, I have identified organizations that have captured some of the elements of a sense of belonging. I am sure that there are many more companies that have embarked on the beginnings of a Belonging Experience (REIT, Prada Epicenter Store, and Niketown come to mind), but I have identified just a few of the many initiatives as examples here, including Apple Stores, ING, TD Waterhouse, Second Cup, RBC, Color Your World (CIL Stores), Running Room, and consumer packaged goods brands, such as Dove.

Each of these organizations has initiated some element of the Belonging Experience, fueled by the various factors identified in the previous chapters. It is quite interesting to note that the majority of organizations that have evolved their brand to engage their customers as part of a community have been either technology companies or financial institutions. In reviewing the progress of experiential retailing, we can identify a continuum over the past decade that has led to the introduction of ideas that support Belonging Experiences. The transition between experiential retailing and experiences that answer a need to belong has just begun, and the examples being reviewed only touch certain elements of what has been defined as the ideal experience. Apple and Dove are the only brands that fully leverage all key elements of the Belonging Experience model.

When reviewing these examples, I have identified the following insights:

1. Knowledge is a powerful tool to unite a community.
2. Hunger for self-actualization drives the need to connect.
3. Disruptive innovation answers the need to belong.

In the following pages, I have identified how these brands have leveraged a sense of belonging in order to help build a framework for the new Belonging Experience model.

APPLE

Insight: Disruptive innovation (humanized technology) answers the need to belong.

Apple stores have become the symbol of innovation. The recent flagship Fifth Avenue store, with its iconic glass cube, was the company's 147th, with others scattered throughout the United States, Canada, Japan, and the UK. The retail strategy was born out of the need to create a bricks-and-mortar experience that leverages the ideal platform to share knowledge and understanding. Ron Johnson, Apple's senior vice president for retail, said he believed the high level of service played a key role in the success of the stores, which generated $115 million in profits for the organization and currently retains the highest sales per square foot of any retailer.

"The idea is that while people love to come to retail stores, and they do it all the time, what they really appreciate the most is that undivided personal attention," Mr. Johnson said. The result is far fewer qualms among consumers about paying premium prices: $30 for an iPhone case, $200 for an iPod Nano, or $1,200 for a computer. Apple stores encourage a lot of purchasing, to be sure, but they also encourage lingering, with dozens of fully functioning computers, iPods, and iPhones for visitors to try for hours on end.

The policy has given some stores, especially those in urban neighborhoods, the feel of a community center. One analyst sums up the stores' success this way: "Everything about it works. Whenever we ask consumers to cite a great retail experience, the Apple store is the first store they mention," said Jane Buckingham, president of the Intelligence Group, a market research firm in Los Angeles. "Basically, the people who work there are cool and knowledgeable. They have the answers you want, and can sell you what you need. Customers appreciate that." Even the fact that they can e-mail you a receipt makes you feel like you're in a store just a little bit further ahead of everyone else. The staff, the store, and the products all focus on building a Mac community of people seeking to join an organization that celebrates simplicity and innovation. The Belonging Experience designed by Steve Jobs and his design team is all part of an integrated approach that ensures a consistent message. In support of its interactive store experience, Apple's iTunes online music library, MobileMe e-mail network and user-friendly web hosting and blogging tools help maintain and foster a network of like-minded consumers. Each works at reinforcing that Apple is a unique, innovative, and networked organization.

The perception of knowledge as a product is another key factor that leverages an experience of belonging. The "Genius Bar" is a key element of the store where customers gain knowledge and resolve issues with a well-trained professional. The Apple flagship stores also provide auditorium-style training presentations on key software programs. A poster outlining the hours of presentation is also featured at the store entrance. Celebrating the sharing of knowledge that corresponds to the different needs of consumers is a key belonging insight that can be derived from Apple.

SECOND CUP

Insight: Hunger for self-actualization drives the need to connect.

From a humble beginning in 1975 as a shopping mall kiosk that only sold whole bean coffee, Second Cup has become the largest Canadian-owned specialty coffee retailer. And since its inception, Second Cup has grown to more than 360 cafés across Canada and over 15 cafés internationally, making Second Cup a second home to hundreds of guests every day. The company initiated an extensive rebranding exercise that identified key consumer needs that were not being met by competitors and that played to the organization's strength. From these insights, a "Neighborhood Oasis" was created that answered consumers' needs for comfort and relaxation while building on a sense of community. This sense of community was greatly enhanced by the use of a fireplace, plush seating, and a brand myth based on the franchise ownership structure and philanthropic support the organization has provided to the estates growing their products.

Since 2003, Second Cup has opened cafés in Dubai, Kuwait, Lebanon, Oman, Qatar, Saudi Arabia, Egypt, and Turkey, with more cafés planned for Saudi Arabia as well as new ventures in Bahrain, Jordan, and Syria. Second Cup's recent success in the Middle East is based on thorough market intelligence, strong local partnerships, a unique customer experience that leverages an image of being truly Canadian, and the ability to adapt its delivery system to suit local needs. For example, the iconic fireplace has been replaced with a waterfall in the hot-climate market. The image Second Cup fosters is locally owned, yet uniquely Canadian. By franchising each outlet to a local person, the Second Cup brand is tied to the local community, differentiating it from large corporate entities that simply move in and open their doors.

"We encourage our local franchise partners to be like mayors of their communities, taking part in local events and raising funds to support local causes," said Mark Cunningham, vice president of operations and café development for Second Cup International. "We also hold events, such as Terry Fox runs and Canada Day celebrations, in each café to promote our Canadian brand."

Cunningham said that Canada, in and of itself, is a strong brand; and he makes every effort to tie his company's image to it. Café decor features lots of red and white, maple leaf art panels, and even an adapted graphic with a maple leaf rising out of the steam from the coffee cup. The menu also offers beverages with a Canadian twist, such as the Maple Latte. Determining the key elements of community and belonging that can be leveraged as part of the facility is an important lesson that can be learned from Second Cup, along with the integration of the ownership and philanthropic aspect of the brand as part of the brand myth.

TD WATERHOUSE

Insight: Knowledge is a powerful tool to unite a community.

TD Canada Trust is TD Bank Financial Group's customer-focused personal and business banking business. Serving more than 10 million customers nationally, TD Canada Trust provides a full range of financial products and services through its retail branch network comprised of over 1,100 branches. TD also provides its customers with leading edge telephone and Internet banking and through access to more than 2,500 "TD Green Machine" automated banking machines. TD acquired Waterhouse Securities in 1997. The brand originated as a U.S. discount brokerage firm. The name TD Waterhouse was formed and was used for TD's British, Canadian, and U.S. brokerage activities. In Canada, TD

Waterhouse thus replaced the brand Green Line. In order to effectively differentiate the brand from the current and potential competitive entries and to become more accessible to consumers wanting to enter the self-directed online investment segment, Shikatani Lacroix developed a unique, engaging client experience that made understanding online investing easy and approachable. With this in mind, the project's overriding objective and premise for the new retail experience was to capture the essence and spirit and encapsulate the overall excitement of an actual stock-market trading floor.

To achieve this, a unique retail environment was created, with a major focal point that created interest and excitement for consumers, in the form of a central "Info Hub" for the DIY investor. This area is the meeting point for a myriad of technologies, all created for gathering information on various stocks, markets, and funds, which is showcased in one central area.

The area includes a central hub of TV monitors, showing the various global exchanges and/or financial/business channels. In addition, market indicator boards are situated on three-sided displays, along with interactive display terminals. Supporting this central area are knowledge pods that are used for demonstrating the ease of use of the online program. The area also includes a reference library for annual reports and corporate videos, in addition to books and reference material for investments. Comfortable seating is also available to invite clients to stay and spend their time reading pertinent information. Private broker offices in addition to meeting rooms are located around the perimeter of the space to allow for a higher level of intimacy and privacy.

The facilities were also designed to be flexible, with a key seminar area at the front of the store, highly visible from the street. This area hosts weekly investment seminars and presentations from various investment consultants. The belonging insights that can be derived from TD Waterhouse is that active participation, the excitement of real-time trading, and the provision of high-tech tools all help drive a client's emotional bond to the retail experience. On-site expertise and easy access to information stimulates curiosity, interest, and a high propensity for a return visit.

ING

Insight: Hunger for self-actualization drives the need to connect.

ING is one of the world's largest financial services organizations, operating in sixty-five countries. The organization positioned itself as the rebel financial institution, allowing its customers to save more while being in greater control of their financial life. ING had identified that it lacked a physical presence in the marketplace since the majority of its sales and marketing efforts was done over the phone or on the Web. They realized that a physical presence would promote building relationships with potential customers who tended to be younger consumers entering their equity-earning years.

The new facility aligned the banking shopping experience with a café experience, offering guests the opportunity to watch television, read books and magazines, or surf the Web, all the while enjoying a premium coffee offering. The various flagship stores were located in high-profile urban centers in major cities around the world.

Merging interactive technologies with larger-than-life graphics, convivial information pods, and a seminar room, the store divided the floor into the café service counter, comfortable café-style seating area, and an area to conduct conventional banking with dedicated tellers. The environment made it easier for customers to explore the full range of services being offered by the company. Web-surfing kiosks were located in the center of the store to allow greater access to information on the Internet.

A choice of stylish finishes and colors helped create an inviting, warm, engaging atmosphere unlike anything found at other bank firms. For more private conversations, the facility featured two separate but open offices with comfortable chairs and round tables. The belonging insight that can be derived from ING is that key learning from the premium café sector can be mimicked to create a unique experience. In addition, emotional signing can be leveraged to link the benefits of the services with consumer needs, while technology can be integrated as part of the facility while still ensuring privacy.

RBC

Insight: Knowledge is a powerful tool to unite a community.

The Royal Bank of Canada is Canada's largest company. It has over 1,400 branches across Canada, over 70,000 full- and part-time employees worldwide, and offices in over 34 countries. Its master brand RBC is used on all its business units. In Canada, the bank is branded as RBC Royal Bank, a combination of its new master brand and its traditional Canadian brand. Examples of its brands include investment banking division RBC Capital Markets, full-service investment brokerage firm RBC Dominion Securities, and online investment site RBC Direct Investing. RBC also has a large retail banking presence in the southeastern United States, marketing itself as RBC Centura, which will be called RBC Royal Bank (USA).

In 2006, RBC initiated the development of a new consumer experience model that clearly identified the need to evolve the experience beyond the conventional transaction model in order to reinforce the company's position as "Trusted Advisor." My firm worked with RBC to create the new consumer experience based on key insights gained through extensive research using Hotspex proprietary research tools. These insights leveraged key hidden needs that the current financial institution network was not meeting and that consumers felt were of the greatest importance.

The new experiences found a happy balance between consumers' need for privacy and speed of service with those that define knowledge as a key product. The main lobby area serves as a learning center that features curved privacy walls, comfortable lounge chairs, and a reference library of pertinent financial information, in addition to a TV featuring investment news and information. A community bulletin board is mounted to the wall and is clearly visible within this area. The learning center also integrates a greeter station to provide a high level of service and access to an RBC representative for clients with questions or needing assistance. New office designs were created to reinforce a level of collaboration and the ability to provide personal service while allowing for a heightened sense of privacy. The staff lunchroom was enlarged to allow for staff training and team-building meetings. The in-store communication is simple and clearly reinforces the "First For You" brand position.

The RBC example shows how creating a learning center as part of the branch experience is a more economical and quicker-to-market approach. By integrating a learning area, a high level of service and access to information were achieved, and warming the overall decor with wood and natural materials and soft seating created a more inviting environment.

COLOR YOUR WORLD

Insight: Hunger for self-actualization drives the need to connect.

Color Your World has over eighty years of experience in the paint and wallpaper industry. Starting in 1912 as a small family-run business, the original store was located on College Street in the heart of Toronto. Until 1967 the company, under the name

Tonecraft Paints Limited, was a major supplier to thousands of painting contractors across Canada.

In the 1990s the chain identified the potential opportunity to service the do-it-yourself (DIY) home decorating market, and the owners developed a completely new merchandising concept. Under the name Color Your World, the company repositioned itself for selling decorating products directly to the DIY customer.

The new store design, created by my firm, leveraged a key insight: Consumers do not buy paint or wall coverings. They purchase solutions to their creative needs for a home that represents their personal self-image. A key factor in this solution-based purchase process is the need for knowledge. With so many choices to decorate a home, consumers are overwhelmed and have a high degree of anxiety in the selection process. The store layout was created to allow for mix-and-match tables with access to a wide range of books, samples, and ideas to help ground consumers' choices and ease the selection process. The merchandising is grouped around projects, and the endcaps are devoted to the idea or technique of the month. Everything about the store reinforces learning and knowledge with the cash centrally located to provide ease of access from all corners of the store.

In order to simplify the process, Color Your World developed decor themes around four color concepts that were explained as part of the paint wall and key literature. A wide range of room setting examples were featured in all four color schemes to allow for a visual representation of the full creative potential. Wall and window covering samples and books, accent material, and flooring samples were integrated as part of the mix-and-match tables. The back of the store features a seminar area with weekly hands-on workshops available for consumers wishing to learn about a specific paint or decor technique.

Color Your World's success demonstrates the importance of clearly defining the customer's true need, simplifying the decision process, leveraging knowledge and learning as a strong value proposition. The company's success has been derived from thinking beyond the product to integrate the need for knowledge as part of the store environment. In addition, changing the focus of the sales process from product transaction to consultation creates a connection with the consumer.

THE RUNNING ROOM

Insight: Hunger for self-actualization drives the need to connect.

Rounding out the case studies is a chain that has truly embraced the meaning of a Belonging Experience. When it comes to offline community building around a brand, there are very few as successful as the Running Room. This retailer has truly leveraged the offline success into an equally persuasive online offering. The Running Room is an Alberta company, which originated in 1984 out of founder John Stanton's wish to purchase quality running shoes from someone knowledgeable about the sport. John, who began running in 1981, found the quality of service in large sporting goods stores was very poor and the staff (usually on a commission basis) were anxious to sell the most expensive, rather than the most appropriate, shoe to customers. The chain is North America's largest specialty running and walking retailer of sporting goods, apparel, and footwear, operating ninety-two corporately owned stores from coast to coast. The Running Room is expanding throughout Canada and the United States. Every Sunday morning at eight o'clock, outside of every Running Room outlet everywhere in North America, runners meet to warm up for a run with their designated "community."

The chain appeals to a wide range of runners. Whether they are slow 5Kers or marathoners in training, they have a community of like-minded people waiting to run at the Running Room. The Running Room sells a running lifestyle and backs it up by fostering an active community that lives this brand and congregates around its properties. In short, the Running Room is everything that an online social network aspires to be, supported by a physical presence. Their site does a great job of reinforcing their core offline values online, and it is a good example of a company leveraging its core strength through its online property.

The Running Room home page drives you immediately to the key content areas for its community (not its commerce): the "events" page, the community "forum" page, the "photos" page, and other important pages designed to get you to put down the Cheez Doodles and go for a run. Their stores are smaller than the big box formats so that they can be more accessible to people walking to the store prior to and after their run. (This is especially smart since they are ahead of the curve as it relates to sustainability, allowing their customers to access the store on foot.) The environment is simple and easy to shop, with brochures and information boards featuring their run times.

To follow in the Running Room's footsteps, organizations can learn that if you sell community—not a product—loyal sales will follow. By creating an integrated experience based on group needs (walkers, novice runners, active runners, and serious marathon runners), the physical experience can expand beyond the store and can be a pathway to linking communities.

DOVE

Insight: Hunger for self-actualization drives the need to connect.

Belonging Experiences can migrate beyond the realm of retailers and service providers. The Dove Campaign for Real Beauty is a great example of how a packaged goods company has leveraged a very effective integrated campaign to create an engaged community. Through consumer research, Unilever identified that women felt intimidated and depressed when they compared themselves to typical models with perfect bodies in the media. Their advertising and marketing team responded by showcasing real women with real curves in their TV and marketing programs. In support of the communication plan, Unilever also launched a Self-Esteem Fund to help free the next generation from self-limiting beauty stereotypes with a goal of reaching 5 million young women by the end of 2010.

The program actively seeks participation and involvement from consumers. As part of the overall campaign, a series of photographs were featured as part of a traveling exhibition in North America where famous photographers captured everyday women. The exhibit was part of a grassroots campaign to gain understanding and knowledge about the issue. The Web site was also an integrated part of the program, featuring educational information and a quiz regarding confronting and conquering women's biggest beauty hang-ups and fears.

From Dove's success, organizations can learn to identify a key insight that is not being met by other brands and that is meaningful to consumers. The next step is to create an integrated experience based on a deep emotional need by identifying how the physical experience can expand beyond the store through the use of traveling exhibits, in-store merchandising, and events, such as fashion shows. The Dove campaign is another shining example of how knowledge can be leveraged to stimulate engagement and support.

CHAPTER FIVE
THE BELONGING EXPERIENCE MODEL

In the previous chapters, I have identified the underlying factors that are driving the need for customers to belong and the ways organizations have started to create experiences that leverage knowledge as a key currency. Most current service and retail models focus on the functional (how does it perform?) and emotional (how does it make me feel?) dimensions, which provide limited opportunities for differentiation and momentum for brands. Both the functional and emotional factors have become the cost of entry in today's marketplace. To truly build a circle of trust, organizations need to evolve their offering to reinforce the aspirational (how does it empower me?) nature of consumer needs in a way that is fully integrated at all consumer touchpoints.

Creating an experience that leverages an unmet empowering consumer need will create trust (it's all about them) in a Belonging Experience that will be hard for competitors to match. I have identified this new belonging model to help organizations build communities through the use of the acronym ACT, which reinforces the fundamental steps consumers take to develop a relationship: attract, connect, trust. The model explores how each of these steps can be leveraged to evolve from a functional or emotional nature to an aspirational dimension that shifts the value equation to include a strong sense of control and knowledge. The use of ACT as a verb (to take action according to key insights) and also a noun (a main division of a play or performance) reinforces the duality of the Belonging Experience. Since the process includes a physical asset, the acronym leverages the stage and plays metaphor, where the physical setting is the backdrop to the performance, setting the stage for the act.

ACT also represents the actual performance by actors, which is the new experience model, including the customer and the staff as active participants in the play. The verb "to act" also talks to the action-oriented nature of building a trusted relationship and the fact that creating this relationship is not a passive process and involves various actions along the various steps of the relationship process.

The following pages outline my consumer experience mapping model and processes to assist your organization by

- helping to deliver a brand experience that appeals to the cognitive, rational, and emotional dimensions of the customer's needs.
- attracting, connecting, and establishing trust with the core target group in a way that helps differentiate your offering from competitors.
- establishing full integration as part of your corporate culture and operational strengths of the organization.
- creating unique brand relationships that will allow your organization to retain the best customers and, as a result, be able to charge more, sell more, more often, generating stronger profits.

Implementing the ACT consumer belonging model will also build stronger brand equity, propelling the future profit potential, driven by the loyalty customers have to the brand while fully leveraging the brand equity in meaningful and new ways.

THE BELONGING RIPPLE FACTOR

Similar to what happens when a stone is dropped in a still pond to create pulsating ripples, the service model acronym ACT is divided into six core factors that spiral outward to an emotional and aspirational ripple (Exhibit 2):

Aware: Create an impression in the blink of an eye that gives the brand permission and credibility to sell knowledge as value.

Attract: Provide an environment that helps reinforce the value proposition while laying the groundwork for a sustained relationship that builds toward sales and profitability.

Communicate: Develop tools that allow for a sustained relationship beyond the purchase.

Connect: Create an experience that allows for a comfortable and effective transaction for both the customer and the staff.

Transact: Ensure the experience. Branding and tools help in the sharing of control and the knowledge process.

Trust: Establish a relationship and not just a transaction. This is part of how the experience needs to act as the bridge between consumer needs and those of the organization, building trust through consistent performance and living the brand promise.

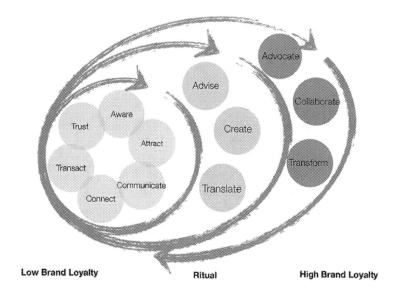

Exhibit 2: Belonging Experience Model

The challenge in evolving the ACT Belonging Experience beyond customers' functional needs is to identify the answers to the following key questions:

- What are the various consumer touchpoints with the brand, and how do they influence perception and reinforce the brand promise?
- What steps do consumers take, and what are their sequential values? How do they differ pending consumer target group profiles (men and women, young and old)?
- What are the hidden needs that are not being met by the current consumer experience, and how can these be leveraged to create a true brand community?
- How can the various stages/processes help build a total consumer experience that is meaningful and fully integrated?

- What are the ideal communication tools and their levels of importance at each of the moments of truth, throughout the ACT process?
- What aspect or type of knowledge has significant value to customers that currently is being undervalued or not leveraged?
- What behavioral changes are required by the frontline staff to ensure a strong sense of belonging and community?

DEFINING VALUE

The ultimate goal of the ACT model is to assist organizations in getting to the aspirational outer ring (illustrated in Exhibit 2). The surest way to achieve this is to redefine the value proposition. A customer value proposition consists of the sum total of benefits that a company promises a customer will receive in return for the customer's associated payment (or other value transfer). In simple words: value proposition = what the customer gets for what the customer pays. Accordingly, a customer can evaluate a company's value proposition on two broad dimensions with multiple subsets:

- Performance: what the customer gets from the company relative to a competitor's offering
- Cost: financial and access investments

The company's marketing and sales efforts offer a customer value proposition; the company's delivery and customer service processes then fulfill that value proposition. In a Belonging Experience, value is derived from the combination of the tangible and intangible factors. I have identified tangible factors as the actual cost for the service or product, the functional benefits, how it performs following purchase, consistency, reliability, and quality. The intangible aspect represents the total customer experience, which includes the aspirational benefits the actual product/service provides in addition to the level of acknowledgment and service.

A case in point is BMW and its value proposition. You could argue that BMW's value proposition is engineered performance, and consumers are willing to pay a premium for this feature. However, the true value of BMW is not based strictly on the tangible but how this brand mirrors their buyers' aspirational self-image. A BMW represents the way the buyer's image is projected through the car as a youthful, energetic, and responsive leader.

In order to provide a strong value, brands need to evolve beyond the performance-driven features to a new level, which includes the overall emotional and aspirational dimensions of the experience. Another aspect of the experience portion of the equation is the rise of the importance of knowledge as currency and power. The new value proposition needs to factor in how knowledge and understanding play a critical role in enabling customers' self-actualization. It is this self-actualization that provides the greatest influence on the ultimate value for any brand.

Part of the experience is the ability to provide customers a level of control over their decisions that reflects their need for growth and understanding. This control can come from better information prior to and during the transaction, to how they actually transact. With the rise of vigilant networks, the importance of allowing a shift of control to the customer as part of the value equation is paramount. Which part of the consumer experience can we delegate or share control over? How can we leverage knowledge as a tool to allow the social network to support your brand and experience? These are key questions that need to be explored as part of the overall process.

New Understanding of Cost

On the cost side of the equation, there are both the financial and cost dimensions. Price is defined by the amount of money the customer is willing to pay for the product, while the cost identifies all of the variables in receiving the given service or product. Typically, cost translates into convenience and level of service as part of the purchase process. Time factors are another critical element in the cost equation and, with the rise of time pressures on consumers, brands that truly help get the most out of a given job do extremely well. Just look at the rise of convenience packaged foods, which demand a high retail price. Another challenge in developing a Belonging Experience that fosters a community is ensuring a high level of transparency on the price and cost side of the equation. From an execution standpoint, the way the cost converts to social and cultural issues has a huge implication on the actual value established by consumers.

The rise of the need for sustainable products and organizations and the concerns of how corporations are impacting developing-country citizens are now just a few of the factors that form part of the new value equation.

For an organization to truly create a vibrant, engaged community, it will be critical to include the social impact of the organization if a high level of transparency is to be achieved. Another consideration in the value equation experience component in allowing brands to create a sense of belonging is the need for customer acknowledgment.

Acknowledgment evolves beyond the transactional process of physical recognition typically found in how staff members are trained to greet guests, to a more aspirational level of defining products that acknowledge the hidden needs of customers. In some cases, the need for recognition is manifested in the offering of products that are tailored to unique self-actualization needs and the way information and knowledge are shared between the organization and the communities they serve. On a more physical level, the actual design of the facility recognizes the different needs of its customers well beyond the requirements of handicap access criteria. Finally, acknowledgment needs to provide the tools for customers to translate the information and products into empowerment to create wealth and security and foster a strong sense of belonging.

CHAPTER SIX
NOT ALL MOMENTS OF
TRUTH ARE EQUAL

Have you ever waited in line for a service or had to go through numerous telephone prompts just to get to someone who could answer your question? While you were waiting, did your perception of that company change? How open were you to listening to a marketing message? These situations are common and define one of the many points of contact customers have with brands. These moments of truth are key in defining whether your brand loyalty chain is strong and the organization is truly living up to the brand's promise of consistent performance. In order to ensure strong brand loyalty in a market where consumers are skeptical and struggling to be in control, organizations must better anticipate and integrate the right consumer experience at each of the key touchpoints that support the various moments of truth.

Jan Carlzon, president of Scandinavian Airlines, coined the phrase "Moments of Truth (MOT)," as he described what occurs when customers come in contact with companies and experience various degrees of quality. Mr. Carlzon noted that a positive MOT with a customer builds brand loyalty and repeat purchase, while a failed MOT creates dissatisfied customers who look elsewhere to get their needs met.

Underlining the importance of creating an effective MOT is the heightened need to avoid damaging a brand's reputation and allowing disgruntled customers to become brand detractors, communicating their wrath on YouTube, Facebook, and other highly visible social networks. MOTs are the critical moments when your brand needs to deliver on its promise, consistently and based on a defined level of expectation from customers, irrespective of whether the given moment is being managed by another organization, such as a retailer, or through the infrastructure of the given company. The need to develop a clearly defined MOT is emerging as a key competitive advantage for marketers wanting to gain strong customer loyalty and a clear point of difference in the marketplace by converting customers to advocates for the brand. With the advent of the Web and the shift of control from the marketer and retailer to the consumer, this need to clearly map out and manage the entire customer relationship at all touchpoints has become paramount.

An IBM Global Business Services white paper identified three simple guidelines that apply to each and every customer interaction:

- Delight customers when it makes sense (and cents).
- Fix where the company fails on its promise.
- Adjust the delivery when an interaction doesn't matter.

Historically, MOT opportunities were focused on organizations that have a physical presence in the marketplace, such as retailers, service organizations, and financial institutions. With the introduction of the Web and alternative channels of distribution, the importance of understanding where your brand is delivering an MOT that meets these guidelines has evolved to include packaged goods organizations and companies that rely on distributors and retailers to sell their product.

ENSURE A STRONG RELATIONSHIP

The challenge for marketers, retailers, and operators is to define which of these MOTs carry more weight and impact in fostering the right relationship and which are in a supporting role that may have little to no influence on the ultimate relationship. Most organizations that have explored MOT strategies focus on transaction-focused touchpoints, where the different stages of customer interaction with the brand are clearly defined with a set of metrics that are financially or functionally driven. (For example, did you serve the customer in under one minute? Was the offer clearly communicated? Did the salesperson respond to the customer's need?)

Although this approach is still relevant today, I would like to evolve the thinking in order to take into consideration a much wider and more balanced view of the ideal MOT by understanding which of these moments has the most impact and value to the organization in fostering a strong sense of belonging and customer engagement. In addition, I have explored further understanding of how to best integrate elements of the marketing mix to best support the MOT. To accomplish how organizations can identify which MOT is critical in engaging the customer and promoting brand loyalty, I have identified a new perspective that should be taken into consideration as you align the right level of importance of your Belonging Experience touchpoints with that of your customer needs. I have redefined the MOT acronym to include this new perspective as part of a relationship equation:

Customer Loyalty = $\dfrac{\text{Belonging Experience}}{\text{Defined Moments of Truth}}$

Consumers today are looking for far more personal contact from highly emotionalized, living brands that require marketers to develop new levels of intimacy. Part of this intimacy is allowing consumers to play a stronger role in the relationship and desired experience with the brand. It is this Belonging Experience that allows consumers to truly engage with brands by giving them a sense of control. A key factor in fostering this Belonging Experience is the ability to both cognitively and emotionally connect with consumers throughout the brand experience, at each critical moment when the relationship is being created and maintained.

MOMENT OF TRUTH ALIGNMENT

The first step in understanding the right hierarchy of importance for each MOT is clearly understanding the type of experience your customers fall within, allowing the marketer to adjust the MOT experience at different levels of the interaction with the brand. Through my consulting practice I have noticed that leading organizations are constantly striving to find the right balance among managing each consumer touchpoint, the allocation of the right level of resources for every customer MOT, and the level of marketing activity against each of the consumer segments. To help explain the relationship among these factors, I have outlined below an MOT alignment pinwheel to assist in the process. In the following pages, I will elaborate on the definition and relevance of each of these circles of influence and how to best develop the ideal MOT experience across the various consumer touchpoints.

The pinwheel (Exhibit 3) defines three driving factors that impact the relevance and importance of each given MOT. The outer circle identifies the various touchpoints that consumers leverage to foster a relationship with a brand. They range from areas controlled by the consumer (social networks, product/service usage) to those managed by the marketer. The second circle of influence represents the persona types that reflect the behavior and attitudes of consumers. These range from task-oriented behaviors to those rooted in more aspirational needs. The final outer circle of influence represents the dimensions of experiences that customers desire as part of their relationship with the brand. The alignment of each of these points within the circles of influence will assist in defining the right hierarchy of importance for each MOT in creating brand loyalty.

THE DIFFERENT DIMENSIONS TO A BELONGING MOMENT OF TRUTH (MOT)

The most effective approach to understanding which of these key MOTs creates a Belonging Experience that fosters strong loyalty to the brand takes into consideration that most consumers enter a relationship based on cognitive, rational, and emotional needs. These needs consist of trade-offs between functional requirements versus consumers' needs for belonging based on feeling valued and their level of confidence, knowledge, and security. I have conducted numerous consumer attitude and behavioral studies to understand what drives customer loyalty. What I have learned by analyzing the data from a wide range of industries and markets is that the way consumers judge the right MOT is directly reflective of the type of relationship they want from that given brand, at that given moment. My research also pointed to the fact that these behaviors represented the same customer at different types of need. By clearly understanding the balance between these needs and how they impact the relationship between brands and consumers, we are able to effectively align the right emphasis on the MOT with the right level of resources and processes. Based on my experience working with thousands of brands in all sectors of the industry, I have identified the following three basic relationship models (Exhibit 3) based on a customer's need for a Belonging Experience that range from a functional to more emotional context.

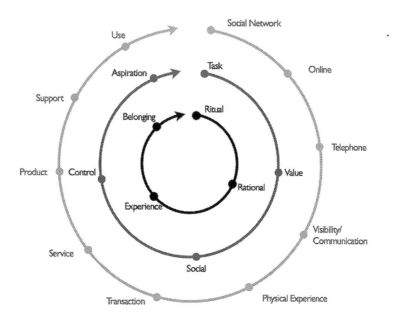

Exhibit 3: MOT Experiential Pinwheel

Exhibit 4 clearly identifies the four typical quadrants of customer needs that must be taken into consideration when aligning the organization's resources against the right MOT. Most sales processes can be divided based on the customer's functional and emotional needs across a task-oriented or experiential-driven experience. For example, paying bills at the local bank would be defined as a repetitive transaction that has a functional, process-driven need. Functional transactions with a high experiential dimension represent experiences that tend to be purchase-intensive but where the actual overall shopping experience factors, such as ambiance, play a critical role. Shopping for groceries or books would fall within this category, where part of the value equation for the consumer is the actual experience.

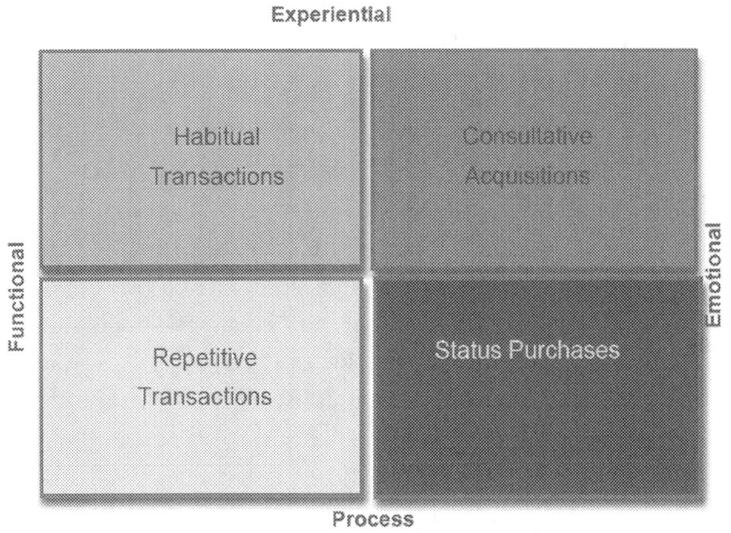

Experiential

Habitual Transactions	Consultative Acquisitions
Repetitive Transactions	Status Purchases

Functional / Emotional

Process

Exhibit 4: Engagement Matrix

Shopping experiences that tend to be process-oriented and incorporate a high level of emotion represent transactions where the given product or name of the retailer plus the level of personal service tend to play a critical role in fostering the relationship. Shopping for clothes, cosmetics, or automobiles falls within this category since the products being purchased are tangible assets.

Highly experiential shopping that has a high emotional dimension tends to represent transactions where knowledge and advice (intangible assets) are the products. The acquisition and planning of investments, seeking medical advice and services, or retaining the advice of legal council would fall within this category. Each one of these quadrants has a significant impact on how best to deliver the right MOT.

Jean-Pierre Lacroix

THE MANY PERSONAS OF A CONSUMER

The second dimension of the MOT pinwheel explores the different personas that consumers can take on pending their given needs. The term "persona" comes from a Latin root, literally meaning "the masked character in a play," and it defines the role that the character has adopted as part of the scene. In the context of the MOT, the mask represents the customer's behavior, while the play represents the given situation as part of the shopping experience. It has been noted that the same consumer can have different personas with the same brand at different times during the given relationship or given part of the day. A case in point is banking, where consumers will act very differently when they want access to their money versus negotiating a loan or requesting investment advice.

Although the brand has not changed, the persona has changed based on the consumer need, impacting how they define their MOT. Each of these personas has different behaviors that impact the given MOT as part of a given brand. In the following pages, I have outlined the five typical types of personas based on how these personalities align with functional and emotional needs against the type of transaction (Exhibit 4) and the impact that each has as part of the various MOTs. It is important to understand that demographics or social standing does not typically define personas but rather the role they play in the desire to fulfill a need. Since digital technology has started to play a critical role in building relationships and shifting the control back to consumers, I have considered the way technology has impacted the various persona behaviors and the various areas of opportunity for marketers.

THE TASK PERSONA

A typical challenge for brands arises when customers' behavior is on autopilot and they are going through the service motion without paying much attention to the surroundings. This type of relationship typically reflects a grudge purchase, such as paying for gasoline or bills, and tends to be focused on accomplishing a simple task. The typical persona in this type of relationship is focused on the need to complete the task in the least amount of time and at the highest level of convenience. Examples of task-oriented persona purchases include paying bills at banks or utility companies, paying for gas, tollbooth transactions, checking in at the airport, and cash withdrawal at ATMs.

This type of relationship is driven by MOTs that ensure the process remains simple, fast, and focused with the least amount of barriers. In this group, MOTs are not required to have staffed service since the need for speed and simplicity trumps the desire for intimacy. Currently organizations that have staffed services are replacing these with a technology process (airline check-ins or grocery store automated checkouts), since the time and expediency overrides the need for personal service.

The key MOT for this type of customer starts with the lineup and ends with the transaction. Of all of the MOT scenarios, this type of behavior is the most concentrated in the key areas that establish the level of loyalty and brand preference. The key MOT touchpoints focus on online systems that are easy to understand and use and customer service that requires the least amount of time. Humanized services are not as critical if the task can be automated or completed through the use of technology.

Only when these areas do not work will this type of persona require the assistance of personalized service. Banks have realized this need by having the ATM at the entrance of branches, quickly accessible to customers. Service stations ensure that their retail footprint is small and offer multiple pay points situated adjacent the door. The introduction of pay-at-the-pump RFID technology is a great example of meeting this persona's need for speed.

With this persona, customer lineups, technology, and digital interfaces that are not intuitive, store layouts that are tricky to navigate, staff that cannot direct them to the right location, or too much information at the point of purchase are all negative MOTs that will lead to a bad experience. These consumers are in split-second transaction mode, and anything that slows the process or creates confusion is a serious challenge.

The use of communication for this persona must be focused on the given task, and any additional information that does not enable the effective completion of this task will be perceived as extraneous and contribute to a negative experience.

Financial institutions have considered the use of their ATM screens as a vehicle to create more awareness regarding new services and products. However, a recent study completed for Wells Fargo for their new ATM interface design identified that the single most used feature of an ATM is the cash withdrawal. Consumers didn't notice or use more customized ATM tools unless they were intuitive and automated. Sell messages at the ATM (if being considered) should focus on providing suggestions on how to make these types of transactions more efficient (i.e., "Have you tried our automated bill-payment service?").

THE VALUE PERSONA

A key component to how customers perceive a brand is the value derived from its use. This ranges from more functional needs, such as convenience, ease of use, and reliability, to more emotional needs, such as how the brand makes them feel. Value persona consumers are seeking organizations to validate their decision to select their brands and are typically motivated by the functional side of the decision spectrum, knowing that their decision to purchase a product was primarily based on the rational and functional benefits of the product, while the emotional and status sides of the equation play a far lesser role.

This behavior tends to manifest itself with consumers who are very confident about their decisions and see themselves as savvy shoppers who know how to get the best out of any situation. Brands marketing to the behavioral needs of this segment need to clearly identify the value equation that includes functional, cognitive, and emotional benefits in order for consumers to feel in control of making the right decision.

Discount and warehouse retailers and private label vendors are great examples of marketers catering to these savvy shoppers who are motivated by the hunt for bargains to drive their sense of self-worth. Within this behavior group, the MOTs are focused on messages and shopping processes that reinforce the value equation, from larger shopping carts to wider aisles and visible displays.

MOT interactions with staff are focused on a need base and become critical only when a given product is not visible or within reach. This segment has come to accept that the trade-off for value is inconvenience and a lower level of expert service. Marketers who cater to this type of persona need to focus on more functional and process-driven MOTs beginning before the consumer even enters the store. Factors, such as easily accessible parking and access to shopping carts that are clean and rust-free (since these experiences tend to be found in larger store formats), and interior elements, such as the width of the aisles, the effective use of signing to clearly communicate the value proposition, the ease of navigating the store, and finally, the ease of the checkout process, are all critical to this segment.

In this experience, the key MOTs are driven by experiential factors that rely far less on human interaction, which is not to say that this is not important, but it plays a far less critical role in the average shopper's experience. Conflict resolution, such as returns, handling defective products, or receiving advice on how to find and use products, would form the only critical MOT factors that include the need for human interaction.

Home Depot stores are a great example of this, with their interactive displays, clearly defined departments, great signage, and automated checkouts. The chain has reinforced its customer service and staff expertise with the slogan "You can do it. We can help." But the reality is far different to consumers. The ability for customers to find their given product plays a much more important role in the MOT for this type of behavior, and access to an employee is driven by the need to find the right product. In reality, having access to an associate is less critical for this type of behavior than shopping in a disorganized store with poorly signed aisles.

THE KNOWLEDGE PERSONA

Consumers who are faced with a wide range of options are looking to an organization to provide the right information so that they can gain a better understanding of the right choice. The touchpoints that support a customer's search for information will have a much greater impact on how they perceive the brand. The knowledge persona is emerging as one of the most sought-after and valued target segment for marketers. From the brand credibility information controlled by consumers through social networking sites to the various brand touchpoints controlled by the marketer, such as the Web site, in-store communication, and product information, the need to clearly help consumers access the information they require as part of a manageable process is critical.

The key factor for organizations to appeal to knowledge-seeking consumers is the ability to provide access quickly, efficiently, and honestly to this group while creating a platform through expertise to expand the knowledge offering well beyond the brand's requirement. This group of consumers is seeking knowledge based on trust and credibility. Ensuring that your organization provides a transparent approach to providing access to knowledge will ensure that you maintain the preferred brand status. Financial institutions, drugstores, and now medical centers are emerging as areas where MOTs supporting the access to knowledge has become critical.

If the task experience tended to require very concentrated MOTs, the knowledge experience has the broadest number of MOTs that have a significant impact on how consumers perceive the brand. The underlying factor is the need to gain relevant knowledge that will assist this type of customer in making the right decision. The knowledge experience starts well before the purchase process since the actual value for the brand is not its functional benefits, but those that reinforce a sense of knowledge. Whether it be the way consumers can get more out of a given product or how they can be empowered to make better decisions on investments, gaining a strong understanding is critical.

The decision process and the supporting ability to gain understanding and information become the critical factors in defining the right MOT. In this type of experience, the Web site plays an important role and is the first critical MOT. The Web site's ease of use, type of information, ability to search, and relevant and up-to-date content set the customer's first impression when determining if your brand is worth further commitment.

A key area of opportunity for a wide range of organizations and a key MOT opportunity is the queue process. In most instances, consumers' main focus is to ensure that they are in line so that they can complete their desired transaction. Most organizations understand that wait times seem shorter if distractions, such as TV programs and magazines, are available. However, in my opinion, this is a significant lost opportunity for this group since they are predisposed to gain knowledge and understanding, which is truly lost waiting in line.

A great case in point is the use of computer terminals in bookstores to allow customers the opportunity to search for a given book and identify its availability within the store. Not only does this technology provide easy access to a given topic or author, but it allows the user the opportunity to explore books and authors who share similar styles. Consumers are willing to change their typical behavior of scanning for books at the shelf level for the use of technology since they understand that the desired outcome will be more efficient while allowing for a greater level of knowledge transfer.

Bank One tested television merchandising programs in eleven of its thirty Milwaukee locations, with the ability to customize its retail messages according to specific branch needs. The programs retain a 70 percent viewing rate among customers while enhancing the bank's paper-based merchandising program, since video has the ability to tell more of the story and people are more willing to watch.

Harris Bank, a division of Bank of Montreal, implemented a similar program in 2003 and has documented that customer recall of product messages proves 7 percent higher in branches that employ digital signs than in those that do not. In addition, bank representatives note that people refer to digital display messages when inquiring about product offerings.

THE SOCIAL PERSONA

In today's time-deprived and socially structured environment, consumers are seeking to connect with others in order to feel valued. Brands that provide a social structure for people to connect need to clearly understand how consumers interact with their brands and why. Great examples of social doorway brands include Starbucks and Dunkin' Donuts or smaller brands, such as Second Cup and Caribou Coffee. These brands create an environment conducive for people to meet, mingle, and socialize outside the office or home environment. Panera Bread is another chain that has built a strong reputation as a business meeting place, with comfortable booths and free Wi-Fi access.

Several years ago, my firm was retained to reinvent a major casual dining chain that had lost its way and competed strictly on cost. Research highlighted that the true benefit of eating at the chain was what I dubbed "family therapy," since eating out was the only time families actually got together to share events of the week or the month. This raised the questions: What is the most critical moment of truth for this chain? Is it the menu, the server, or the seating and atmosphere of the restaurant?

A recent study: "The dining experience: do restaurants satisfy customer needs," by Tommy D. Andersson and Lena Mossberg from the School of Economics, Gothenburg, Sweden, identified that an ideal experience is more than just the menu. Research results pointed to a total willingness by patrons to pay for a full-fledged ideal dining experience.

There are interesting differences between a luncheon and a dinner in regard to the value that customers place on stimulation. Most striking is the increase in willingness to pay for stimulation of social and intellectual needs (i.e., restaurant interior, service, other guests, and good company) during a dinner as compared to a luncheon. This difference comes out even more clearly when we compare the two types of restaurants in absolute money terms.

Whereas the willingness to pay for physiological comfort (i.e., to relieve hunger) remains virtually the same, the willingness to pay for intellectual and social stimulation increases dramatically; there is a twofold increase in willingness to pay for fine cuisine, a sixfold increase in willingness to pay for restaurant interior, an eightfold increase for good company, and a twelvefold increase in value placed on the importance of other guests. What numerous projects in this sector have demonstrated is that social persona brand experiences are not about the transaction or purchase process, but they are more focused on the environment and experience. Although service levels and quality of food are critical, for most brands, they are the cost of entry.

The key MOT occurs during the queuing process (is it organized and efficient?), at the order desk (Is the server friendly and helpful?), at the menu board (Are the offers clear and easy to understand?) and during accurate execution (Did I get what I ordered?). The seating area is a critical MOT and will significantly impact the overall guest experience and how they define the brand.

My firm recently completed a major rebranding program for a global coffee chain. The learning from the research clearly identified the comfortable soft seating and overall ambiance of the café as being the key unmet consumer need that clearly differentiated this chain from its larger rival. Social persona behaviors are predicated on the need to create an environment conducive for people to meet and socialize, providing the right balance of privacy, intimacy, and visibility. Effectively communicating to this group of consumers tends to reflect the environment and desired experience and, as such, smaller, more personal promotional materials tend to be noticed and read versus large signs.

These consumers are looking for information that will enrich their lives, and storytelling plays a critical role in meeting this need. Communication needs to provide support to maintaining and building the social dialogue within the experience. Since these types of experiences tend to be linked to food and beverage, washroom walls tend to be very effective vehicles in communicating information or promotional messages. Servers and customer greeters play a critical role in the MOT for this persona as a means to gain further information and promotional offers. Other key communication elements consist of social cause or product story posters and cards as part of the product merchandising that draws attention during the transaction experience adjacent the cash.

THE ASPIRATIONAL PERSONA

This behavior is based on how the brand experience mirrors the self-esteem image of the consumer and how the various MOTs foster a sense of recognition. This behavior drives the need to be treated as someone special, cared for, and important. Car dealerships and clothing stores are great examples of environments where the MOT is driven by treating customers as the center of attention throughout the duration of the relationship, from the time they purchase the product to subsequent meetings for service.

The aspirational persona is one of the hardest to market to since all aspects of the MOT are critical, from how the customer is greeted at the door, to the relationship before and after the visit. All are of equal importance and relevance to how customers want to be treated. According to IBM customer experience research, emotional factors are often equal to, or more important than, tactile attributes, from a customer's perspective.

Although reasons for purchase are almost always a combination of factors, in many cases customers attribute emotional reasons, such as dignified treatment, to be as important as fundamental tactile attributes, such as price and quality. Aspirational brand experiences tend to represent products and services that support the consumer's need for self-actualization, and the MOTs are an integral part of the brand's cache. However, there are, within this context, higher impact MOTs, and there is a need to develop a hierarchy of needs in order to effectively operationalize and provide consistency.

For this persona, the key MOTs are focused around the humanization and customization of the service, namely, the ability of the marketer to make each of its customers feel as though they are unique, with individual needs and desires. Leading organizations that I have worked with have leveraged the automated queue system to allow customers to register their interest to receive service as part of a kiosk that is supported by a company greeter. Knowing that they have been identified as part of a queue sequence allows this group the opportunity to seek additional information or specific product information. While we often think of the typical queue as a line of people waiting for staffed service, there are other types of queues that have an impact on the MOT.

For example, a queue might be a cluster of people sitting at computer terminals scattered around the globe waiting for dial-up access from their Internet provider, or people responding to automated voice recognition prompts in order to talk to a live customer service representative on the phone. Each of these consumer virtual touchpoints has a significant impact on how customers will perceive a given organization at that given MOT. Strategies that segment the customers based on the given persona will ensure that in each case, the experience is positive. In the case of knowledge-seeking consumers, the ability to have their questions answered efficiently is critical.

Certain systems allow for customers to identify their given issue using a list of prompted responses to provide quick answers to the most asked questions while reducing the perceived wait times. Digital signage and interactive tools play a critical role amongst this group in gaining access to the desired information. Again, the use of computer terminals in bookstores is a great example of this.

A key to ensuring a winning MOT is the ability of the organization to provide effective tools to assess the needs of and solutions for its customers in a way that allows them greater control and involvement. In this type of persona, the level of privacy and intimacy is critical, while the role of the sales associates needs to evolve to a higher degree of advice and expertise. The ability of the organization to create an experience that is focused on the emotional benefits of the services or products will achieve a greater sense of customer loyalty and higher sales transactions.

The role of technology is to provide a platform for an enhanced level of personalization and customization for this type of persona. Understanding past needs and being able to project future desires and wants are all part of creating MOT experiences that build on the aspirational needs of this group. The key MOT consists mainly of how the persona perceives the level of intimacy and, as such, the environment, the knowledge-based material, and the interaction between the sales consultant and the consumer are critical.

CHAPTER SEVEN
CREATING AN ENGAGED
EMPLOYEE EXPERIENCE

Today's economic climate has heightened employee concerns regarding job loss and cutbacks on workplace benefits. This fear has undermined an organization's ability to engage the workforce as employee focus shifts from the need for advancement opportunities or company culture to financial security. Employers are also challenged as productivity increases and cost control dominate their short-term initiatives, taking valuable resources and a determined focus away from employment branding initiatives.

Organizations need to clearly understand the value of having engaged employees who support the brand promise and align their behaviors to better mirror the organizational values. Numerous research studies have shown that there are direct correlations between staff engagement and the level of customer brand loyalty. A Forrester study conducted in 2008 with five thousand consumers on the correlation of customer experience and loyalty clearly identifies that consumers with good experiences consider purchasing more and typically do not switch brands.

The Verde Group conducted a study for the Retail Council of Canada to determine what makes a "WOW" shopping experience for customers. The study identified that 75 percent of shoppers who enjoyed a great experience with a specific retailer definitely intended to return to that retailer the next time they needed a similar product. When shoppers encounter merely "standard" experiences at a store, their likelihood to return drops by over 65 percent. Key factors that influence how consumers rate a great experience were directly related to the level of engagement by the staff, their ability to be sensitive to customers' time and needs, and their ability to resolve and compensate for customer issues.

Employers remain focused on retaining employees and controlling costs while also addressing employees' diverse needs for security, control, and work-life balance. On the other side of the equation, employees are feeling more stressed and pressured to perform. A survey conducted by the Center for Work-Life Policy (CWLP) identified that between June 2007 and December 2008, employee loyalty plunged by 65 percent, and the number trusting their employers plummeted from 79 percent to 22 percent. Employees also, on average, tend to be older, leading to a heightened need for financial security and control.

A study by MetLife identified that the concern about having a comprehensive financial plan for retirement increased from 53 percent in August 2007 to 58 percent in November 2008, while the younger baby boomers expressed the biggest increase from 56 percent to 67 percent.

Employees which formed part of the study identified that having enough money to make ends meet, having appropriate health insurance for the family, and having job security ranked over 58 percent of their level of overall concerns. A study from the National Institute for Occupational Safety and Health identified that more than 40 percent of workers felt their job was very or extremely stressful. Based on a recent *BusinessWeek* article, employee disengagement continues to be a critical issue across a wide variety of organizations as they work through the economic downturn. The Corporate Leadership Council, a program of the Corporate Executive Board, disengaged 1 out of 4 employees at the end of the first half of 2009, according to a survey of over 61,000 employees.

One of the main causes of this disengagement is directly linked to the massive change employees have experienced when it comes to their Employment Value Proposition (EVP), or the value that employees gain by working for a particular organization. Eighty-two percent of employees indicated that their EVP has trended downward quite dramatically in the past six months due to reasons, such as layoffs, organizational restructuring, and shifts in management. These findings lead to the question: how can organizations ask employees to become engaged and heroes for the brand when they have a high concern for survival and poor EVP perception? The ability to engage employees to share a common vision, when the vision being created is not clear or attainable, is posing the biggest challenge for organizations.

THE SHIFT FROM EVP TO ENGAGEMENT VISION PERCEPTIONS

Organizations have clearly defined brand value propositions that have been translated into an employment value propositions (EVP), a term used to denote the balance of the rewards and benefits that are received by employees in return for their performance in the workplace. However, there has been a missing link between the EVP and actual employee engagement, and much of this gap is attributed to the inability of employees to easily visualize their future. Linking an organization's brand position to the EVP has been the cornerstone in developing employment-branding initiatives that attract the best recruits, motivate the best hires, and ensure the organization is focused on living the brand promise.

Although these achievements are critical to an organization's success, what is unclear is how employees assimilate the EVP proposition in a way that impacts their daily work-life behavior.

Over the years, my firm has been involved in numerous employment branding initiatives in support of new customer experience models, the rebranding of an organization that included a new position and unique selling proposition, and leveraging the existing organization position to better focus the employees to a given direction. Through countless employee interviews and management discussions, I have come to realize that the most powerful tool to engage employees is their ability to visualize the desired outcome for both their careers and the organization.

In their book *The Carrot Principle*, Adrian Gostick and Chester Elton review the results of a 2006 Recognition ROI study that examined 31 organizations and 26,000 employees with respect to the ability of the organization to recognize excellence. The results confirmed our belief that companies providing strong recognition of excellence earned significantly higher return on equity, return on assets, and operating margin. The study also reaffirms my own research that indicated great organizations motivate their employees by tapping into people's aspirational needs as they pertain to their work. In an organization that drives improved performance, the ability of its employees to self-actualize their success is critical.

Many organizations confuse self-actualization with being the rising star, but often this is not the case. While wealthy or highly celebrated people might reach self-actualization, many psychologists believe that most employees who have reached the highest level of happiness are unknown beyond their circle of family and friends. Organizations develop when people are allowed to reach their particular level in Maslow's hierarchy. Once people's physiological needs are met and they feel safe, they begin to support the organization's culture and work toward common goals. History has shown us that the ability of leaders to create real or perceptional images in the mind of their employees or followers has a significant impact on the success of the given initiative. I wonder what would have happened to equality for African Americans if Martin Luther King had not given his "I have a dream" speech, or if Neil Armstrong could ever have taken "one small step for man, one giant leap for mankind" had John F.

Kennedy never shared his vision of putting a man on the moon. These leaders were able to create a visual picture of what the desired outcome would be if everyone worked together, creating a strong platform for engagement.

Organizations, such as Toyota, a world leader in automobile manufacturing, have been able to leverage visuals as both a means to articulate complex employee engagement models as well as a tool to ensure effective compliance by using visual control so that no problem is hidden. The "4P" model of the Toyota Way visually identifies the hierarchy of behavioral importance for each of the four goals of the organization, leveraging learning from Maslow's hierarchy of human needs. At the bottom of the pyramid, Toyota identifies the need for a solid philosophy of long-term thinking. This need supports the right process that produces the right engagement results. This is followed up the pyramid with the behavioral need to add value to the organization by developing people and partners, which leads to the pinnacle need for the organization: the need to drive organizational learning by continuously solving root problems. Another key factor that reinforces the importance of creating a strong visual of the desired outcome is the way employees mirror their self-esteem with that of the organization's perception in the marketplace.

EMPLOYEE SELF-ESTEEM IS INFLUENCED BY PEP

A key to organizational engagement is the degree of alignment of the employee's self-esteem with the perceived external prestige (PEP) of the organization. Based on work completed by Olivier Herrbach, LIRHE, Université des Sciences Sociales, organizational image has mostly been studied using an external perspective focused on strategy and marketing issues. Given its salience in employees' symbolic environment, however, image may also have internal as well as external consequences. A recent study that explored the impact of PEP on three individual outcomes—job satisfaction, effective organizational commitment, and effective well-being in the work environment—shows that all individual outcomes are related to PEP. Mr. Herrbach notes in his study that corporate image should be of growing interest not only to marketing and strategy professionals but also for HR purposes. The major reasons for this relevance of corporate image to HR include the fact that companies are more likely to attract quality applicants if they convey to them a positive image. Organizational image could be helpful in retaining employees, and organizational image is likely to influence employee attitudes and behavior in the workplace through its salience in an individual's symbolic environment.

The study's findings validate the critical link between organizational image and employee outcomes. PEP was clearly linked to job satisfaction, effective organizational commitment, and effective well-being at work.

The findings are further validated by two previous articles that have studied this topic, while extending the findings to both a larger and more diverse population, namely the Riordan study (1997) based on 174 employees from one small U.S. electric utility company, and Carmeli and Freund (2002) research on a sample of 527 management-level employees working in different private-sector organizations. The Herrbach study also tested a differentiated impact of PEP for sales/marketing people versus other managers and found that it was partially supported. This supports the contention that, although relevant for all management-level employees, image issues seem to be stronger for sales and marketing. The study brings into importance how employee self-image is a reflection of the organization's image in the marketplace. The greater the level of positive perception of the organization, the stronger the level of engagement of its employees.

In her book *Foster Success for People: Two Musts for Employee Motivation and Positive Morale Motivation Success*, Susan M. Heathfield notes that people who have high self-esteem are more likely to continuously improve the work environment. They are willing to take intelligent risks because they have confidence in their ideas and competence. They work willingly with teams because they are confident about their ability to contribute. Nathaniel Branden, author of *The Psychology of Self-Esteem* and *Self-Esteem at Work*, also notes that self-esteem is a self-reinforcing characteristic. When we have confidence in our ability to think and act effectively, we can persevere when faced with difficult challenges. The result: We succeed more often than we fail. We form more nourishing relationships. We expect more of life and of ourselves. Image plays a critical role in fostering this self-esteem, and how peers perceive the organization becomes critical.

Finally, a key factor in ensuring engagement amongst employees is the need for understanding. In his book, *The Fifth Discipline, the Art & Practice of the Learning Organization*, Peter M. Senge identifies that the only long-term sustainable advantage is an organization's ability to learn faster than its competitors. A key to learning is the ability of an organization to translate a lot of information into easy terms for its employees, at all levels of the organization. In most instances, the failure to communicate effectively is the lack of sensitivity to the level of employee branding knowledge and terminology throughout the organization. When large amounts of information are not presented to employees in a way that is easy to understand and recall, most employee branding initiatives created to stimulate engagement end up creating disengagement due to the complexity of learning.

Stories and pictures are the most effective tools in ensuring a high retention of complex information. History has shown, from the pyramids to the way children learn to read, that pictures and stories play a critical role in learning. However, seldom are these tools used to align employees on the employee values and vision of the organization other than cliché posters and graphics.

I believe that Toyota got it right by creating an easy-to-understand diagram with four key messages that its employees can easily retain. This is further validated by memory recall research that shows that most humans can best remember three messages, and the rate of retention drops significantly as more messages are added. HR and marketing professionals assigned to helping organizations live the brand promise need to understand how employees retain information and the ideal approach that will ensure a high level of engagement in the actual learning process. Humor and stories that support empathy and the appreciation of the challenges facing the workers in their everyday lives tend to resonate better and, by their very nature, ensure a higher level of message relevance and retention.

It is also important to understand that the ability to create visuals that synthesize the values and vision of the organization supports how we absorb information. Forty percent of all information we retain is driven by our sight, and 80 percent of what our sight retains is color and shapes. Can you translate your EVP program into simple colors and shapes, and will they be simplified in a way that the message is limited to no more than four elements? The challenge I have faced with most of my firms' employee branding initiatives and assignments, where brand experience has been changed and employee processes need to be modified, is the ability to translate the required changes in the simplest, most visual approach. Written exercises or highly image-related communications have been proven to generate the highest level of message recall and information absorption. These are key factors in ensuring a strong understanding of employee branding initiatives.

The Visual Tools for Engagement

Image-driven perceptions help bridge the self-esteem of the employees to the needs of the organization. Visuals help articulate the final destination while creating emotional connections with employees' need for self-actualization. It has been proven in every industry, sector, and category that consumers by nature do not like to read instructions. Have you ever assembled a barbecue or your child's bicycle and ignored the instruction booklet or, if used, focused on the pictorial images versus the words?

Humans by nature learn through visual stimuli, and these processes can be applied to engage employees in support of the desired brand promise. Over the years I have assisted organizations in developing employee branding and worked with other supporting industries that help organizations manage knowledge and behavioral changes. I have identified a range of tools that could be leveraged to gain a higher degree of support and understanding. These tools mirror how employees want to learn and typically represent how the best organizations manage knowledge, leading to consistent execution of the brand promise.

In his book *The Fifth Discipline*, Peter M. Senge notes that the key to the engagement process is employee enrollment in the organization's EVP program based on becoming part of something of their choice. He notes that employees are committed when they are not only enrolled in the branding process but feel fully responsible for making the vision happen. It is the employees' feeling that the vision is as much a part of their self-esteem and their needs as they are part of the organization's competitive requirement. Senge notes that in most contemporary organizations, relatively few people are enrolled and even fewer are committed. The majority of employees are in a mind-set of being compliant, following the rest of their peers in supporting the vision without being fully engaged.

The challenge for managers is to ensure employees are not merely compliant with the organization's vision and mission but fully engaged to embrace both the meaning and the execution. The ultimate desired outcome for organizations is the type of social networking found on such sites as Facebook, YouTube, and LinkedIn, where the participants take an active role and are advocates for the experience, recruiting friends and colleagues to join the social network. I have identified a range of visually oriented tools that organizations can leverage based on best industry practices and my own firm's experience in determining what works and what does not in gaining a stronger employee commitment. I have grouped these tools as part of three categories: gaining meaning, aligning actions, and measuring performance. These three categories best define the various phases of engagement that will deliver meaningful and measurable change for the organization.

Gaining Meaning

Employee Brand Identity

In ensuring a strong understanding of the fundamentals of the EVP program, leading organizations leverage the use of key thematic visuals that capture the essence of the brand story. I have found this practice very helpful in rallying the employees around a common vision and helping link all of the key messaging that supports the EVP program, ensuring a consistent message. I have seen a range of image tools used by organizations, and each has a key common trait. Each of the programs that leveraged a strong image linked that given image to the core brand message and desired behavioral outcome. It is also critical that the EVP identity not become a fad based on the movie of the moment but, more importantly, can last the test of time, providing a consistent frame of reference for the EVP program.

Employee Branding Attributes

One of the most effective approaches in gaining meaning and understanding as part of the employee brand proposition is its ability to be distilled in three key words that support the brand promise and desired employee engagement. These key attributes tend to be action words that predicate a desired change in behavior or the ability to better leverage a current behavior that is part of the equities of the organization. Typically, these words form part of the visual language used to support the EVP program, linking the meaning of each attribute to a desired end state that supports the organization's internal needs. Key EVP attributes need to be carefully chosen, and more importantly, their meaning needs to be carefully crafted in a way that will allow everyone in the organization to share in their meaning.

VIDEO STORIES

We have been trained to learn from stories and visuals, mostly via our home entertainment systems. We can easily recall a given movie sequence or key message since the information being provided is entertaining and provokes an emotional response through the use of actors, stories, and challenges. We have found that one of the most emotional approaches to gaining understanding of an EVP program is through movies. Storytelling is such an impactful way to ensuring information retention, and employees can relate to testimonials of fellow employees or a well-scripted story delivered by actors. Images help crystallize the challenge the organization must overcome as well as the importance of the individuals in meeting this challenge and the desired end state. I am always amazed at how effective this process is to gel the organization. The title of the video story also allows the organization to link the message to other elements of the EVP communication strategy.

SOCIAL MEDIA

Only recently have organizations gone beyond their company intranets to deliver key EVP messaging by leveraging social networks, such as Facebook, YouTube, and Twitter, to harness the social behaviors of their employees. A conference held by *Fortune Magazine* identified that organizations were just starting to leverage the full power of Twitter as a vehicle to deliver pertinent company information. Companies have banned the use of Facebook to minimize the time employees spend browsing the Web versus working, but employers are realizing that these social media outlets can be effective tools in the distribution of information and building brand loyalty. The key challenge of leveraging this emerging technology is the organization's ability to control the information being distributed. Many organizations are reviewing both their legal requirements as public organizations and the privacy issues to determine how best to capitalize on these new social tools.

Gartner released a report in May 2009 that identified the approaches companies were adopting for using Twitter for business purposes. This research narrowed down the three main ways that companies are using Twitter today:

- Direct: as a marketing or public relations channel, much like an extension of their corporate blogs, posting corporate accomplishments and distributing links

- Indirect: employees "tweet" instead, enhancing their own personal reputations and, in exchange, supporting the company's reputation

- Internal: used internally to share ideas or communicate about what projects they're working on

Microblogging sites designed for businesses are also being leveraged. Yammer and Presently are two of the top options for a Twitter-like platform for the workplace. My firm has harnessed the power of the blogosphere from IBM to create customized blogs for our TeamClient Project Management System.

ALIGNING ACTION

A key to the success of any program is ensuring the organization's actions support the EVP program values and beliefs while also ensuring ongoing awareness and commitment.

BEHAVIORAL MODEL MAPS

Mapping through the use of diagrams is an effective visual tool in gaining internal alignment. Some organizations consider these maps to be employee value proposition models, while others define them as scorecards that align with key metrics. Irrespective of the term used, the purpose of this given tool is to visually represent the desired organizational need as part of supporting behaviors, all of which are defined by how they align with the overall vision. Models also tend to give context to what the organization wants to achieve by linking the activities of each functional area to the common vision of the program, thus ensuring that the silo structures of most corporations are effectively aligned. Behavioral model maps tend to also support the on-boarding and re-boarding processes and allow the organization to translate the key elements from the map to given strategies and tactics required to support the common vision. A map's true value is to provide the organization with the ability to chart its progress and identify its destination well before it takes its EVP journey.

ONLINE DIGITAL LEARNING TOOLS

I have had the opportunity to work with firms, like Fifth P Solutions, which specialize in providing organizations with online learning tools, such as tests and quizzes, to sharpen the level of knowledge and ensure consistent delivery of the message. For large-scale organizations where the manager's primary role is not that of an educator but one that manages the resources and equities of the company, teaching may not be a core strength.

How, then, does an organization with thousands of employees effectively communicate the brand message and meaning while remaining consistent in its delivery?

Online learning tools, such as those provided by Fifth P Solutions and other leading learning organizations, form part of the core competency of the corporate communications department. These tools provide a great platform to move the burden of consistency from the manager to the technology while still allowing managers to effectively monitor and manage the learning process. Online systems are a great resource for employees to learn more about the employee brand while fostering a learning culture where information can be absorbed at a comfortable rate over a period of time.

OFFICE ENVIRONMENT

The office environment is one of the critical behavior enablers for organizations wanting to align their EVP with their employees' daily routines. It has become common practice to either change or find new office environments as a result of a merger or a restructuring. However, very seldom does an organization leverage its physical assets to create a canvas to communicate its EVP program on a daily basis.

I have gained some important insights with respect to the importance of the work environment through my firm's collaboration with organizations considered to be some of the best employers around. From large-scale organizations, such as TD Bank, PepsiCo, and Petro-Canada, to small yet successful firms, the learning is the same.

The common trait for all is the importance they place on leveraging their work environment as a physical manifestation of their EVP program, from staff lunch and meeting rooms to halls and main building entrances. Some have gone as far as building office TV networks to keep everyone informed on the progress of the company and acting as a reminder of the role everyone plays in living the brand promise. Others play on-boarding videos in their main lobbies for new suppliers and visitors to the company, outlining the organization's beliefs and values.

PERFORMANCE VISIONING TOOLS

The use of employee visioning tools is an effective way to help each contributor to identify its desired personal outcome, from both a career and personal development perspective. Smart organizations have realized that employees who can visualize their futures are those who can fully commit to the success of a company's vision. These tools tend to link the EVP program beliefs and principles to those of the employees' self-image. Some provide personalized vision cards that employees carry in their purses or wallets. Others have even gone so far as to implement this tool as part of the employees' computer screen saver, replacing the generic computer-supplied home screen with one that reinforces the EVP.

RE-BOARDING PROGRAMS

In support of online learning tools, organizations should also initiate quarterly re-boarding programs that leverage learning tools and knowledge sessions with either their immediate managers or, in some cases, the leaders of the organization. If geographical distances are an issue, these sessions can be conducted via videoconference and supported by workbooks to ensure the quarterly activities and performances align with the EVP.

MEASURING PERFORMANCE

As the saying goes, "What gets measured gets done." This is especially relevant in the context of EVP programs. The ultimate yardstick for how an organization embraces its EVP program is the metrics for how the leadership defines success. The following outlines some of the visual tools that successful organizations have embraced to ensure a high level of staff engagement.

Public Performance Charts

Many organizations post their quarterly performance and company objectives on large charts located throughout the workplace. Successful management teams have come to realize that such visual tools are great in harnessing the energy of the organization for a common performance goal. However, very few companies I have worked with have identified the EVP performance metrics, other than featuring industry awards and other external performance signals. If employees are to commit to an EVP program, it is important that the performance metrics are visually communicated in easily accessible vehicles.

Company Pledge

A visual representation of a company pledge helps to engage employees and serves as a reminder of the EVP. I assisted one of North America's leading office supply companies in a reengineering of its customer experience as part of a new business approach that increased the value proposition to home offices and small office business customers. A key to the new experience was a commitment to sustainability for the entire organization. In order to make this commitment a visual manifestation, the leadership of the organization created a large mural where each employee and supplier signed his or her name in support of the new initiative. The pledge wall became a key element in the company's offices and a reminder to all of the focused commitment.

People Recognition Symbols

Many organizations feature plaques and employee achievement awards in their lobbies. These symbols of performance harness a sense of commitment to the organization but tend to be sales-focused rather than an indication that these individuals have lived the brand promise. I would argue that some of the recipients have done nothing to enrich the organization in leadership that would motivate others to follow.

However, I was impressed by one of my clients who publishes and distributes yearly performance books to the entire company. The performance book contains not only hundreds of photos and stories of people who live the brand promise, but it also provides stories of their commitment. The true value of the book is in its message that any individual can contribute to the success of the brand promise, irrespective of the tenure and level within the company. This approach supports many employee engagement studies that identify that recognition for a job well done is more important than a raise. I wonder, if this is the case, why so few companies celebrate the success of people who deliver on the brand promise at all levels of the organization and not just sales.

It is no wonder that this organization has won the J.D. Power Customer Service Excellence Award five years in a row and is one of the most preferred companies to work for in North America.

Employee Performance Charts

Employers and employees dread yearly reviews, and very few are inspirational or can effectively motivate employees to grow or align their performance with the EVP program. In most cases, performance reviews are driven strictly by the financial and performance needs of organizations. However, great organizations that effectively support their EVP program clearly align the performance of the individual with the employee need for empowerment and growth. The real opportunity is to deliver these via highly visual metrics, such as career dashboards, that graphically represent the individual's performance.

Why not consider using the same graphical interface people have become accustomed to when driving their cars on the daily journey to work? How difficult would it be to apply this same visual language to employment performance? We all know what it means to be running on empty and to be driven beyond our limits, or how it feels when the engine needs a tune-up. Would it be so difficult to apply this same daily logic to business? Most organizations have spent millions of dollars on company performance dashboards, but the employee dashboard is missing from the whole equation. I believe that smart organizations realize that what helps guide people to drive to work could be the same visual language to drive their career and commitment to the company.

CHAPTER EIGHT
THE PATHWAY TO ACTION

In assisting organizations in developing Belonging Experiences through the ACT model, I have identified a pathway that will guide you through the different processes, action items, and milestones. Each step builds on the cumulative understanding and knowledge gained in each sequential step, allowing your organization to evolve your learning and build consensus along the journey. The pathway is divided into four key steps:

STEP ONE: IDENTIFYING THE VISION

The goal of this step is to clearly articulate a potential vision, based on insights, that would form part of the new experience and that impacts each of the ACT elements. Creating a visual manifestation that defines potential scenarios the organization needs to explore allows a range of potential ideas to be integrated as part of a learning and alignment process. In addition, the first step in the process is to gain internal alignment with the establishment of a project team and charter.

Step Two: Defining the Value Proposition

Based on the consumer and staff insights and consumer validation of the various scenarios, a clearly articulated value proposition emerges that supports the final vision. The elements of the value proposition should impact and better define the ACT elements. This step also includes the identification of key metrics, which will define success for the organization.

Step Three: Creating the Story

The best way to communicate an idea is through a story that paints a clear picture of the overall experience and factors that are influencing both the internal resources and the external communities. The story is both narrative and visual and allows the reader to fully grasp the potential of the vision.

Step Four: Implementing the Story

The final stage of the process puts the vision into action through a series of strategic imperatives that are implemented by the various disciplines within an organization. These imperatives evolve all aspects of the consumer Belonging Experience at each brand touchpoint. The ultimate outcome of this phase is a clearly defined narrative and illustrative story told through the eyes of the community members.

Putting the Process into Action

In the following pages, I have outlined each of the four steps, broken down into tasks that will assist your organization in understanding how to create an effective Belonging Experience.

The process is designed in a way that allows each organization to customize the process to its specific needs (i.e., an organization may have already established an effective value proposition and, hence, the process would facilitate validation and further considerations). Finally, this process is iterative, with adjustments and modifications to the ideal experience based on learning and insights gained at the completion of each consecutive task.

STEP ONE: IDENTIFYING THE VISION

In order to determine where you need to evolve the customer experience, it is necessary to gain a thorough understanding of the organization's capabilities and to identify the potential customer need.

CREATING THE TEAM

The first step in the process is to create a cross-functional team whose members will lead the project. From this group, a project champion will need to be assigned for whom the given assignment will become the focus of his daily activities. You will need to establish weekly or bi-monthly meetings with set times and places.

FORMULATING A PROJECT CHARTER

As part of the mandate, the team will be empowered to develop a project charter that will clearly identify the project outcome, timelines, and investment, in addition to key objectives and resource requirements. It is critical that the project charter be broad and focused on a hypothesis in order to not confine the final outcome without clearly understanding the true nature of the opportunity. The project charter should gain endorsement and approval at the senior leadership team level to enlist their support when the project nears implementation and rollout.

THE DISCOVERY STAGE

The next step is defining the ideal vision of the new Belonging Experience, which will consist of identifying all pertinent available information on the consumer, competition, company, and category. This will form part of an extensive discovery stage that will provide the team with the appropriate level of knowledge and understanding. This stage should also list all of the missing questions that need to be answered as part of future studies. Finally, this step will gain additional insights from customers and employees on the key attributes that are driving the category, differentiating the organization, and providing value. This stage should incorporate the processes outlined in chapter 3, "Brand Engagement."

As part of this stage, I recommend the initiation of the RACE evaluation process to identify key opportunities that leverage the insights identified as part of the discovery stage. The process would include consumer research to determine the stated and hidden drivers for the category that are not being currently met by the organization and its competitors. This type of research will also provide an understanding of the real competitors for the customer's attention and loyalty.

DEFINING THE SANDBOX

Before the process can start defining the vision, it is important to clearly understand the real problem and factors driving the issues, by addressing the following questions:

- Identify the real problem: What is the major issue to resolve using the ACT elements? This process needs to dig deep into determining the real problem that needs to be solved. A well-defined problem leads to an insightful solution.

- Define the effect: Why do we need to resolve the problem?

- Review available facts: What do we know already, and what do we still need to discover? What are the hidden and stated drivers that need to be considered, and how do they cluster around the ACT elements?

- Identify your perception: How do people feel internally? How are you viewed externally?

Describe your organization's future when this problem is resolved. What is the vision? What are the four words that define the parameters of this vision? These four words identify the perimeter dimensions of the brand sandbox (the defined extremities of the vision, clearly identifying what is out of bounds) and allows for a strong foundation for the next stage.

CREATING THE SCENARIOS

As part of this stage, it is important to clearly identify the key communities your new experience will cater to and attract. This process should include a clear articulation of the community's profile, size of market, purchase behavior, need, and aspirational desires that motivate them to become engaged. Once you have clearly defined your desired target communities, it is now time to develop a range of scenarios.

Typically, the scenario planning process explores ideas that, at one end of the spectrum, build on the current capabilities of the organization, while at the other end, explore totally new opportunities. I have found this process enables organizations to identify the true edge of the opportunity and discover how best to lead the customer through change. Building on the sandbox definition, the process should explore a range of scenarios that would be taken into consumer validation. The scenarios should conform to the different elements of the ACT model to assist in fully integrating all aspects of what would create a community of advocates.

Validating the Ideas

This stage of the first phase should consist of ensuring stakeholder input and validation through the use of research. The various Belonging Experience scenarios, which are articulated through a narrative story and visuals, should be reviewed as part of quantitative online research. The findings would allow the team to clearly understand how the various ideas connect with customers and staff and which part of the experience helps build an engaging community. It is important to note that these scenarios touch on all potential aspects of the ACT model, including processes, products, people, and positions, to name just a few. References to cost or price would not be covered, since these are best evaluated as part of the actual prototype program.

Putting the Vision into Focus

Based on input from the research, a final draft vision and Belonging Experience articulated through all facets of the ACT model would be formulated with supporting rationale from the validation and discovery stages. The draft vision needs to also identify areas that still need validation and clarification, either at the story or the implementation stage. This stage starts identifying the various factors that are driving value for the brand that will be further articulated as part of the next phase.

Alignment of the Team

The final stage of this process is the alignment of the team to ensure the given draft vision meets all of the project charter mandates. Typically, this process would culminate in a series of internal stakeholder presentations to gain support and understanding on the reasons behind the given direction. It is recommended to leverage these meetings as a vehicle to gain additional insights and to gauge the level of resistance to the new idea. This will allow the team to build key assumptions and perceptions from the organization into the scenario stage.

STEP TWO: DEFINING THE VALUE PROPOSITION

LEVERAGE LEARNING, FINDING THE GAPS

The first task in defining the value proposition for the new experience is to clearly understand to what degree this proposition needs to evolve from the current way of thinking. The research findings should assist your organization in formulating a new value proposition that is better aligned with the new consumer experience while building on your core organizational strengths. To migrate to your new value, it is important to gauge the gap between your current and future proposition through a strong understanding of what key elements are driving this value from the ideal experience validated in research. This process should also identify what value your organization can provide that is not being fully leveraged as part of the consumer experience.

REFORMULATING A NEW PROPOSITION

Following the identification of the value gaps, the next step is the articulation of a clear value proposition that supports the new Belonging Experience. Each facet of this proposition, from the experience and performance to the cost side of the equation, needs to be integrated and clearly articulated as it pertains to the ACT model. As part of this value, an order of importance needs to be established to ensure the right emphasis and priorities are aligned, as the ideal vision becomes a reality. The order of importance needs to integrate the various key consumer touchpoints that were identified in the discovery and scenario planning stages as critical to fostering a feeling of belonging and engagement.

The second part of this stage involves the development of key performance metrics that leverage the value proposition as a yardstick to measure the true impact of the prototype in the marketplace.

GAINING ALIGNMENT

Since the value proposition is the foundation of the consumer experience, it is important to gain internal buy-in and support to ensure that all facets of the organization understand the key implications of the program. This stage includes a review of the brand vision in order to make appropriate adjustments based on the value proposition.

STEP THREE: CREATING THE STORY

DESIGNING THE IDEAL VISION

This stage consists of translating the learning and insights, in addition to the value proposition, into a fully integrated consumer experience that leverages each dimension of the ACT model. In order to achieve an experience that leverages knowledge, engages the consumer, and builds loyalty, the story needs to be written from the customers' perspective, in their words and outlining the entire consumer experience. The narrative needs to integrate all of the various facets of learning established in the previous phases while building on these to reflect the reality of the marketplace. Typically, designing the ideal vision will require several iterations as part of the development stage and should include a clear direction for the communication and marketing elements, while still allowing flexibility to integrate the learning as part of the final support materials. The final outcome of this stage is a narrative and visual manifestation of the ideal vision articulated through the words of your key community.

DEVELOPING AN ROI MODEL

Following the development of the narrative, it will become critical for the organization to articulate a clear return on investment (ROI) model that will support the desired need for change. It is also important to note that this ROI model is based on business assumptions and key learning established throughout the process and will require final validation as part of the prototype stage. The ROI model will also help further define the value proposition in order to clearly understand the cost side of the equation.

INTEGRATING THE GREATER TEAM

It is critical for the leadership team to engage its marketing, design, and advertising partners in order to bring the final vision to life. Consider this phase the next chapter in the book, allowing further clarification and focus on how the ideal vision becomes a reality. Emphasize developing and integrating the acquired knowledge from all of the various phases, in addition to ensuring the right level of emphasis based on what best supports the consumer experience.

HUMAN CAPITAL INTEGRATION

In addition to external partner involvement, this stage should include input and further elaboration of how the new vision will be integrated as part of the HR, operations, and field support areas of the organization. An evaluation of the current hiring, training, and sales support practices will need to be undertaken.

A factual assessment of the organization's ability to undertake the implementation of the new vision should be initiated, and potential gaps that need to be filled prior to the initiation of the prototype should be identified. This stage will culminate in a final training program and selection of the prototype team and location.

Town Hall Meetings

At this juncture of the process, it is critical for the new vision and program to gain alignment with both the leadership team and the in-market team, which will form part of the prototype implementation.

Step Four: Implementing the Story

Putting the Vision to the Test

The final stage of the process is the implementation of a prototype that integrates most of the learning and assumptions built throughout the various stages. As part of the implementation plan, it is critical that the market selected can easily be isolated from a marketing investment standpoint. I also recommend that both a prototype and control site form part of the test in order to gain valuable benchmarking data that can assist in the final analysis stages. It is important that the project team meets on a weekly basis at this stage to ensure all of the implementation issues, as they arise, are dealt with quickly.

VALIDATING THE RESULTS

I recommend the use of ethnography and the initiation of exit research several weeks prior to and after the implementation of the prototype to gauge customer reaction to the changes and gain key learning on what is working and what is not. As part of the analysis portion of the test, it will be important to evaluate sales data, support, frontline staff input, and the findings of customer research to fully integrate all potential learning. Following the prototype test, it will be important to reevaluate the value model and ROI to determine the success of the program and identify the elements that will need to change on a move-forward basis.

INTEGRATION OF LEARNING

Based on the key findings, a guideline will need to be developed to clearly identify each element of the experience. This guideline should articulate in great detail all facets, both tangible and intangible, that will influence the ability of the organization to roll the program out across the entire network. Since the overall process is iterative and knowledge will continue to be gained as new locations are converted, it is important that the guidelines remain fluid and are reviewed quarterly to ensure their relevance.

TOWN HALL MEETINGS

Following the implementation of the prototype(s), it is important to share the program's successes and areas requiring improvement with the organization. It is at this point that the leadership team needs to gain support and final buy-in for the new consumer experience model. This phase of the process is one of the most critical, since, at this juncture of the program, the ownership of the opportunity needs to migrate from the project team to the daily operations of the organization.

The strategies I have outlined will give you the tools to lay the groundwork for a successful transition for your company and brand. The processes can be adapted to fit each organization's specific needs, but the basic framework remains the same. By understanding how consumer needs are evolving, creating an experience to meet these needs, leveraging technology, establishing an employee value proposition, and engaging your employees to live the brand promise, you can create a successful Belonging Experience for your brand that will truly resonate and connect with consumers and positively impact your organization's bottom line.

About the Author

Jean-Pierre Lacroix
President, Shikatani Lacroix Design, Inc.

Jean-Pierre Lacroix is the cofounder of Shikatani Lacroix, a branding and design firm that specializes in integrated design solutions for corporate, packaging, and retail/environmental clients. An honors graduate from the Graphic Design Program at Sheridan College (Ontario, Canada), Mr. Lacroix has developed a reputation as a true innovator and first-rate problem solver, with an expertise in providing clients with unique and results-driven solutions to their product and service needs.

Jean-Pierre was the first, in 1990, to coin and then trademark the Blink Factor formula, which lays the groundwork for consumer interaction with brands and helps determine the key factors that steer consumers toward a particular brand over another during the purchase process. He also coauthored *The Business of Graphic Design: A Professional's Handbook*, which contains valuable information for professionals who hire and work within the graphic design industry.

An Ottawa, Ontario, native, Jean-Pierre resides in Toronto, Ontario, with his family. He has served on many industry association boards, as president of The Association of Registered

Graphic Designers of Ontario, president of the Design Industry Advisory Committee (DIAC), and board member of the Society of Environmental Graphic Designers (SEGD), in addition to director of the Packaging Association of Canada. An accomplished and dynamic speaker, he has lectured at numerous conferences across Canada, the United States, and South America on the subjects of branding and design trends. His presentations have always received high appraisals for content, energy, and takeaway actionable information.

References

Cohen, Marshal. *Why Customers Do What They Do.* New York, McGraw-Hill, June 2006.

Davis, Stan, and Bill Davidson. *20/20 Vision,* Pocket Books, U.S., May 1992

Friedman, Thomas L. *The World Is Flat: A Brief History of the Twenty-First Century,* Vancouver, Douglas & McIntyre Ltd., 2007

Horovitz, Jacques. *A Dream with a Deadline,* New York, Prentice Hall, January 2007

Kitayama, Shinobu and Dov Cohen (Eds.). *Handbook of Cultural Psychology,* New York, The Guilford Press, 2007

Letts, Lori, Patty Rigby, and Debra Stewart. *Using Environments to Enable Occupational Performance,* Thorofare, NJ, Slack Books, 2003

Lovell, Nadia. *Locality and Belonging,* London and New York, Routledge, 1998

Nadeau, Raymond. *Living Brands,* New York, McGraw-Hill, 2007

Nyren, Chuck. *Advertising to Baby Boomers,* Ithaca, NY, Paramount Market Publishing, 2005

Olivier Herrbach and Karim Mignonac. "How Organisational Image Affects Employee Attitudes." Université des Sciences Sociales, Toulouse, France: *Human Resource Management Journal,* Vol 14, no 4, 2004.

Oldenburg, Ray. *The Great Good Place,* New York, Paragon House, November 1989

Schmitt, Bernd H. *Customer Experience Management,* New Jersey, John Wiley & Sons, 2003

Trendwatching. *2007 Annual Trends Report.*

Senge, Peter M. *The Fifth Discipline. The Art & Practice of the Learning Organization.* New York, Doubleday Books, a division of Random House, Inc., 2006

Aguirre, DeAnne, Laird Post, and Sylvia Ann Hewlett. "The Talent Opportunity."
Strategy + Business, Booz & Company September 2009.

MetLife Employee Benefits 2008 Study.

Steven J. Stein, Ph.D. *Make Your Workplace Great: The 7 Keys to an Emotionally Intelligent Organization* , Mississauga, Canada, John Wiley & Sons Canada, Ltd., 2007

Temkin, Bruce D. *A Closer Look at Customer Experience and Loyalty.* Forrester August 4, 2008.

Discovering "WOW" – A Study of Great Retail Shopping Experiences in North America 2009 Verde Group, The Jay Baker Retailing Initiative at the Wharton School of Business and the Retail Council of Canada conducted research to explore the "WOW" shopping experience

Gostick, Adrian and Chester Elton. *The Carrot Principle How the Best Managers Use Recognition to Engage Their People, Retain Talent and Accelerate Performance, Engaging Life-Long Customers, Service and Customer Appreciation,* New York, Free Press, 2007

Executing on a customer engagement model, Adobe Systems

Shea, Linda, SVP/Global Managing Director, Customer Strategies Opinion Research Corporation and Warren Frankel SVP, *The Art of Engaging the Customer: Proactive Steps to Delivering a Differentiated Customer Experience.* Customer Strategies, New York, Opinion Research Corporation, 2009

Using Technology to Engage Retail Banking Customers - Why banks must carefully manage their digital touch-points to create a seamless customer experience by Gallup Consulting Sponsored by Adobe Systems Incorporated

Moll, Julie, Senior Vice-President and Janet Smalley, Vice President of Brand research Marriott VP: *Engaging the customer in a changing market place*, Virginia, Maryland Media, 2007

Beyond loyalty – Meeting the challenge of customer engagement, Part 1, Economist Intelligence Unit, Sponsored by Adobe Systems

Temkin, Bruce, *The 6 Laws of Customer Experience,* New York, Forrester Research, 2006